Sadlier

We Believe™

God Loves Us

Leader's Guide
Grade One

Sadlier

This advanced publication copy has been printed prior to final publication and pending ecclesiastical approval.

About the Cover: The image shows the interior of the Cathedral of the Madeleine in Salt Lake City, Utah. Built in 1909, it is the cathedral of the Diocese of Salt Lake City and the only U.S. cathedral dedicated to Saint Mary Magdalene. It is an example of Spanish Gothic architecture.

For online resources, go to religion.sadlierconnect.com and enter:
Parish/Catechist Access Code: 23BC951JQ
School/Teacher Access Code: 32BCE1LBN

Printed in the United States of America.

is a registered trademark of William H. Sadlier, Inc.
We Believe™ is a trademark of William H. Sadlier, Inc.

William H. Sadlier, Inc.
9 Pine Street
New York, NY 10005-4700

ISBN: 978-0-8215-3071-9
4 5 6 7 8 9 WEBC 21 20 19 18 17

Contents

Welcome to... Sadlier WE BELIEVE

Catholic Identity Edition

This Program will...

* **Inspire, Encourage, and Strengthen CATHOLIC IDENTITY**
* **Foster SPIRITUALITY**
* **Prepare for NEW EVANGELIZATION**
* **CELEBRATE BEING CATHOLIC!**

New

We Believe: Catholic Identity Edition

offers the following:

- There are four *Catholic Identity Retreats* in every grade.
- Every retreat offers prayer, reflection, and meditation on the grade-level themes.
- Retreat themes relate to one of the four pillars of the *Catechism of the Catholic Church* (CCC): **CREED**, **LITURGY & SACRAMENTS**, **MORALITY**, or **PRAYER**.
- Every grade explores the same pillar at the same time, supporting whole-community catechesis.
- *Catholic Identity Retreats* nourish the children's spiritual growth and relationships with Jesus Christ through spiritual experiences.

Catholic Identity Retreats

Each grade level includes four retreats to nurture children's spiritual growth and relationships with Jesus Christ. Designed for use throughout the year in class or retreat-like settings, they offer prayer, reflection, activities, discussion, and meditation focused on grade-level themes. In every grade, the four themes are related to the Four Pillars of the *Catechism of the Catholic Church*—**CREED**, **LITURGY & SACRAMENTS**, **MORALITY**, and **PRAYER**.

Each retreat has six distinct, easy-to-use parts that can be expanded or condensed to fit the allotted time for your program.

Part 1 Children begin by reflecting on the retreat theme in light of their own experiences.

Celebrating Catholic Identity: CREED

Catholic Identity Retreat

Jesus Christ, the Son of God

Part 1 **I Open My Heart**

God the Father wanted to show his love for all people. So he sent his Son, Jesus, to show his love. Jesus is the Son of God.

Jesus was born in a stable in Bethlehem.

Imagine that you visited the baby Jesus. What would you say and do? Add yourself to the picture. Then share what you imagined saying and doing when you visited Jesus.

Grade 1 Retreat: CREED R1

Celebrating Catholic Identity: CREED

Catholic Identity Retreat

Jesus Christ, the Son of God

Part 2 **We Come Together for Prayer**

Leader: Repeat after me as we pray:
Jesus, you are the Son of God. We love you.

All: Jesus, you are the Son of God. We love you.

Leader: Jesus, you are our Lord. We honor you.

All: Jesus, you are our Lord. We honor you.

Leader: Jesus, you show us God the Father's love.
We praise you.

All: Jesus, you show us God the Father's love.
We praise you.

Leader: Sign your name to the note to Jesus.

Jesus, I love you.

Jesus is the Son of God the Father. Jesus taught that God is our Father, too. Let us love God as Jesus taught us.

All: Amen.

R2 Grade 1 Retreat: CREED

Part 2 Children enter into prayer using one of the prayer forms of our Tradition.

Part 3 Using a modified *Lectio Divina*, children reflect prayerfully on a passage from the Word of God.

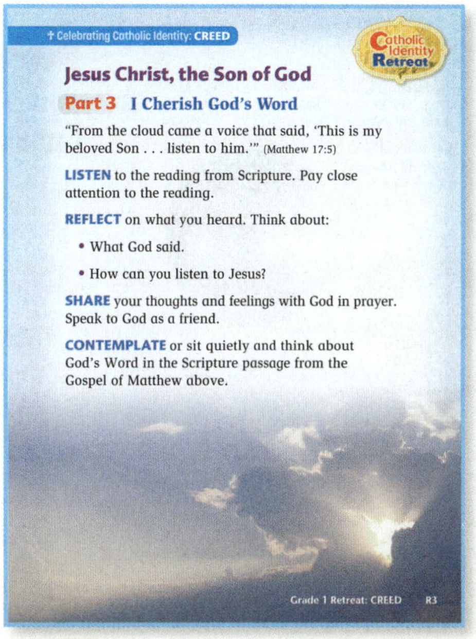

Celebrating Catholic Identity: CREED

Catholic Identity Retreat

Jesus Christ, the Son of God

Part 3 **I Cherish God's Word**

"From the cloud came a voice that said, 'This is my beloved Son . . . listen to him.'" (Matthew 17:5)

LISTEN to the reading from Scripture. Pay close attention to the reading.

REFLECT on what you heard. Think about:

- What God said.
- How can you listen to Jesus?

SHARE your thoughts and feelings with God in prayer. Speak to God as a friend.

CONTEMPLATE or sit quietly and think about God's Word in the Scripture passage from the Gospel of Matthew above.

Grade 1 Retreat: CREED R3

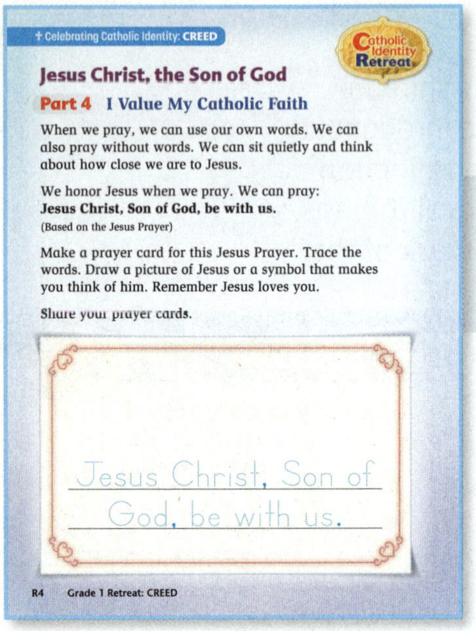
✝ Celebrating Catholic Identity: CREED

Catholic Identity Retreat

Jesus Christ, the Son of God

Part 4 I Value My Catholic Faith

When we pray, we can use our own words. We can also pray without words. We can sit quietly and think about how close we are to Jesus.

We honor Jesus when we pray. We can pray:
Jesus Christ, Son of God, be with us.
(Based on the Jesus Prayer)

Make a prayer card for this Jesus Prayer. Trace the words. Draw a picture of Jesus or a symbol that makes you think of him. Remember Jesus loves you.

Share your prayer cards.

Jesus Christ, Son of God, be with us.

R4 Grade 1 Retreat: CREED

Part 4 Children engage with the retreat theme through activities and sharing.

Part 5 Children celebrate their Catholic Identity through internalizing and expressing their faith.

✝ Celebrating Catholic Identity: CREED

Catholic Identity Retreat

Jesus Christ, the Son of God

Part 5 I Celebrate Catholic Identity

Jesus Christ, God the Son, showed us God the Father's love. Jesus used words to show us God's love. He used actions to show us God's love. We follow Jesus when we love God, love ourselves, and love others.

Together think of an action that answers each question. Take turns acting out the answers.

How do we show that we love God?
How do we show that we love ourselves?
How do we show that we love others?

Grade 1 Retreat: CREED R5

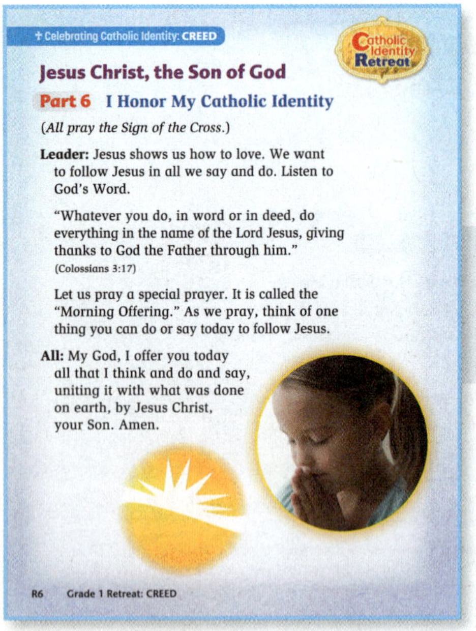
✝ Celebrating Catholic Identity: CREED

Catholic Identity Retreat

Jesus Christ, the Son of God

Part 6 I Honor My Catholic Identity

(*All pray the Sign of the Cross.*)

Leader: Jesus shows us how to love. We want to follow Jesus in all we say and do. Listen to God's Word.

"Whatever you do, in word or in deed, do everything in the name of the Lord Jesus, giving thanks to God the Father through him."
(Colossians 3:17)

Let us pray a special prayer. It is called the "Morning Offering." As we pray, think of one thing you can do or say today to follow Jesus.

All: My God, I offer you today all that I think and do and say, uniting it with what was done on earth, by Jesus Christ, your Son. Amen.

R6 Grade 1 Retreat: CREED

Part 6 Children return to prayer at the close of the retreat with a mission to live their Catholic faith.

Every grade explores the same pillar at the same time, promoting whole-parish catechesis. The spiritual development of the children at each grade level is noted in the Leader's Guide with retreat considerations to help you develop the retreat experience appropriately.

Bringing the Retreat Home

The retreat continues at home where families can share the retreat theme, engage in simple activities, and pray together.

✝ Celebrating Catholic Identity: **CREED**

Catholic Identity Retreat

Bringing the Retreat Home

Jesus Christ, the Son of God

Retreat Recap

Review the pages of your child's *Celebrating Catholic Identity: Creed* retreat. Ask your child to tell you about the retreat. Talk about Jesus:

- Jesus Christ is God the Son.
- God the Father sent Jesus to show his love.
- Jesus taught us to love as he does.

Morning Offering

Your child prayed the Morning Offering in Part 6 of the retreat. Talk with your child about what each of you will be doing this day. Then write your own Morning Offering to Jesus together as a family. Include words that acknowledge Jesus as the Son of God. Ask for Jesus' help to love others as he taught. Pray your prayer together in the morning.

Take a Moment

Your child prayed a form of the Jesus Prayer in the retreat. Pray the full Jesus Prayer together aloud: *Lord Jesus Christ, Son of God, have mercy on me, a sinner.* Pray the prayer several times, meditating on Jesus' love for you. This is a type of contemplative prayer. In contemplative prayer, we simply allow ourselves to rest in the experience of God's loving presence.

Family Prayer

Jesus taught that God is our Father. This evening, talk about people who need God's love. Pray the Our Father together, remembering those who need to experience God's love in a special way.

For more resources, see the *Catholic Identity Home Companion* at the end of this book.

Grade 1 Retreat: CREED R7

✝ Celebrating Catholic Identity: **CREED**

Catholic Identity Retreat

Why We Believe
As a Catholic Family

What if someone asks us:

- How is Jesus Christ both fully human and fully divine?

The following resources can help us to respond:

Jesus Christ is God the Son, the Second Person of the Blessed Trinity who became man. His ministry was filled with not only profound teachings, but also many public healings and even raising of the dead! These miracles and his own Resurrection from the dead confirm his identity as God.

Jesus was also a human person. He was born of Mary and grew up in a loving family in Nazareth. Scripture reveals that he experienced hunger and fatigue and the range of human emotions. He had friends whose company he enjoyed. He needed to take breaks from the activities of life. Indeed, Jesus was not only fully human but is our perfect role model for what it means to be human. He was like us in all things but sin. In this way, Jesus reveals how we are called to lives of faithfulness to the will of God the Father and to love and care for one another, especially those most in need.

What does Scripture say?

Jesus said, "The Father and I are one" (John 10:30).

"[Jesus], though he was in the form of God,
did not regard equality with God something
to be grasped.
Rather, he emptied himself,
taking the form of a slave,
coming in human likeness;
and found human in appearance,
he humbled himself,
becoming obedient to death,
even death on a cross." (Philippians 2:6–8)

The mystery of the Incarnation, the truth that the Son of God became man, is revealed in Scripture and confirmed in the faith of the Church. Jesus Christ is both fully human and fully divine.

What does the Church say?

"For by His incarnation the Son of God has united Himself in some fashion with every man. He worked with human hands, He thought with a human mind, acted by human choice and loved with a human heart. Born of the Virgin Mary, He has truly been made one of us, like us in all things except sin."
(Second Vatican Council, *Gaudium et Spes*, 22, December 7, 1965)

"The Church thus confesses that Jesus is inseparably true God and true man. He is truly the Son of God who, without ceasing to be God and Lord, became a man and our brother."
(*Catechism of the Catholic Church*, 469)

Notes:

R8 Grade 1 Retreat: CREED

Why We Believe As a Catholic Family

This resource for parents presents Catholic teaching and its source in Scripture and Church documents.

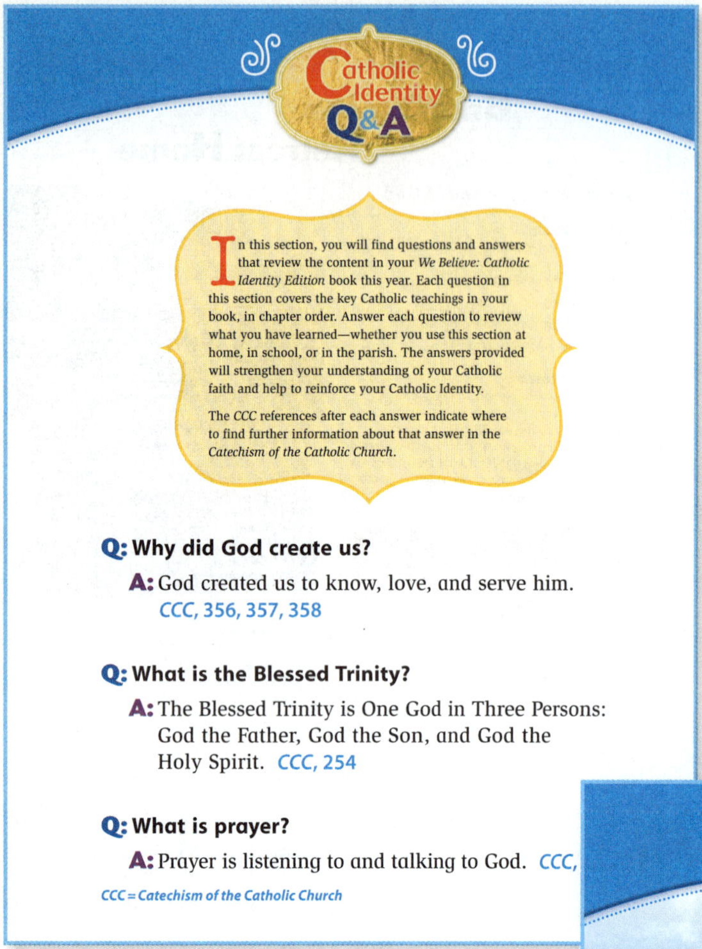

Catholic Identity Q&A

In this section, you will find questions and answers that review the content in your *We Believe: Catholic Identity Edition* book this year. Each question in this section covers the key Catholic teachings in your book, in chapter order. Answer each question to review what you have learned—whether you use this section at home, in school, or in the parish. The answers provided will strengthen your understanding of your Catholic faith and help to reinforce your Catholic Identity.

The *CCC* references after each answer indicate where to find further information about that answer in the *Catechism of the Catholic Church*.

Q: Why did God create us?

A: God created us to know, love, and serve him. CCC, 356, 357, 358

Q: What is the Blessed Trinity?

A: The Blessed Trinity is One God in Three Persons: God the Father, God the Son, and God the Holy Spirit. CCC, 254

Q: What is prayer?

A: Prayer is listening to and talking to God. CCC,

CCC = Catechism of the Catholic Church

Catholic Identity Q&A

Questions are based on what is taught in the student text. Answers are clear and age appropriate.

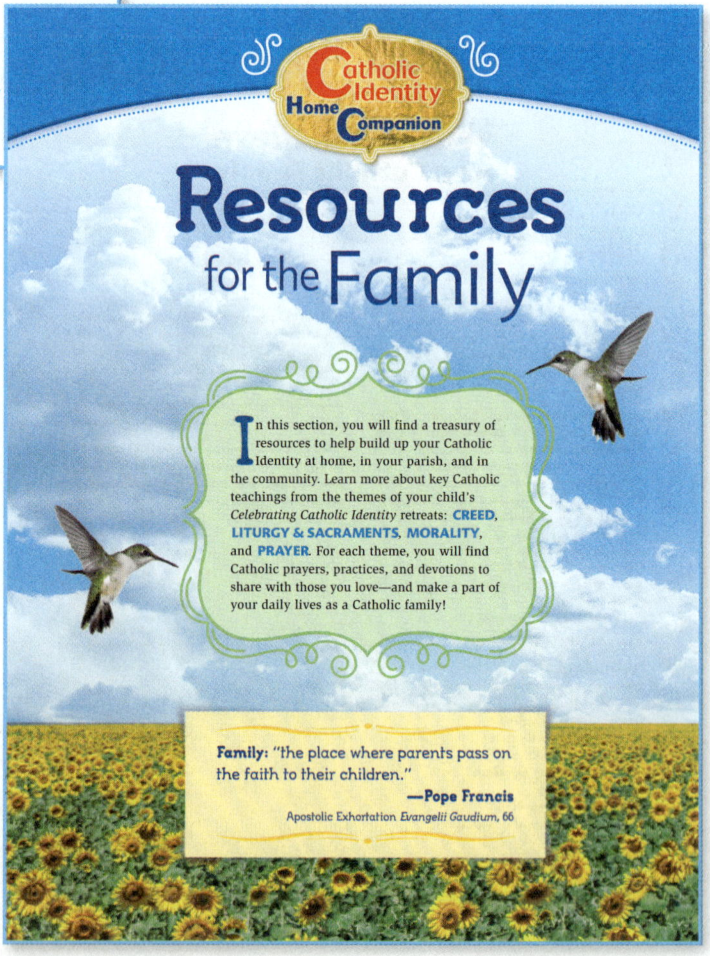

Catholic Identity Home Companion

Resources for the Family

In this section, you will find a treasury of resources to help build up your Catholic Identity at home, in your parish, and in the community. Learn more about key Catholic teachings from the themes of your child's *Celebrating Catholic Identity* retreats: **CREED**, **LITURGY & SACRAMENTS**, **MORALITY**, and **PRAYER**. For each theme, you will find Catholic prayers, practices, and devotions to share with those you love—and make a part of your daily lives as a Catholic family!

Family: "The place where parents pass on the faith to their children."
—**Pope Francis**
Apostolic Exhortation *Evangelii Gaudium*, 66

Catholic Identity Home Companion

Four sections reflect the four pillars of the *Catechism of the Catholic Church* and provide prayers, practices, and devotions to use at home or in class.

Retreat Options to Fit Your Needs

You can expand or condense the *Catholic Identity Retreats* to fit whatever time frame you need. Here's how:

If your time for a retreat is . . .

30 minutes or less, *you can . . .*	45 minutes to 60 minutes, *you can . . .*	1 hour to 2 hours, *you can . . .*
eliminate Part 1 or Part 5.	do the entire retreat.	use the additional resources in the *Retreat Toolbox* and at **religion.sadlierconnect.com** to expand your retreat as needed.

Retreat Toolbox

The *Retreat Toolbox* offers a meditation, a handout, a simple recipe, and a table blessing that you can use to expand the retreats in the student edition.

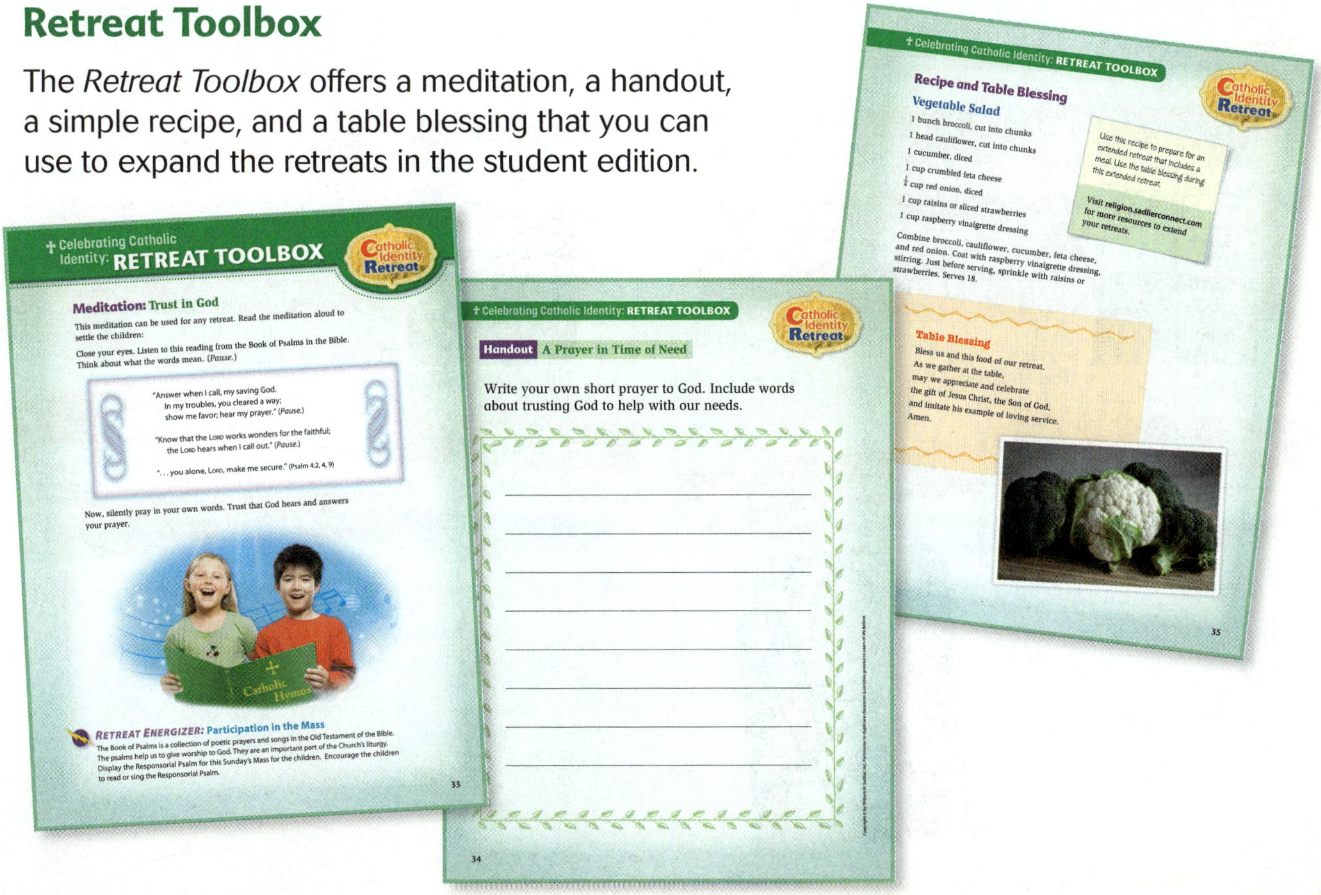
† Celebrating Catholic Identity: RETREAT TOOLBOX

Catholic Identity Retreat

Meditation: Trust in God

This meditation can be used for any retreat. Read the meditation aloud to settle the children:

Close your eyes. Listen to this reading from the Book of Psalms in the Bible. Think about what the words mean. (*Pause.*)

"Answer when I call, my saving God.
In my troubles, you cleared a way;
show me favor; hear my prayer." (*Pause.*)

"Know that the LORD works wonders for the faithful;
the LORD hears when I call out." (*Pause.*)

". . . you alone, LORD, make me secure." (Psalm 4:2, 4, 9)

Now, silently pray in your own words. Trust that God hears and answers your prayer.

Catholic Hymns

RETREAT ENERGIZER: Participation in the Mass
The Book of Psalms is a collection of poetic prayers and songs in the Old Testament of the Bible. The psalms help us to give worship to God. They are an important part of the Church's liturgy. Display the Responsorial Psalm for this Sunday's Mass for the children. Encourage the children to read or sing the Responsorial Psalm.

33

† Celebrating Catholic Identity: RETREAT TOOLBOX

Catholic Identity Retreat

Handout A Prayer in Time of Need

Write your own short prayer to God. Include words about trusting God to help with our needs.

34

† Celebrating Catholic Identity: RETREAT TOOLBOX

Catholic Identity Retreat

Recipe and Table Blessing

Vegetable Salad

1 bunch broccoli, cut into chunks
1 head cauliflower, cut into chunks
1 cucumber, diced
1 cup crumbled feta cheese
¼ cup red onion, diced
1 cup raisins or sliced strawberries
1 cup raspberry vinaigrette dressing

Combine broccoli, cauliflower, cucumber, feta cheese, and red onion. Coat with raspberry vinaigrette dressing, stirring. Just before serving, sprinkle with raisins or strawberries. Serves 18.

Use this recipe to prepare for an extended retreat that includes a meal. Use the table blessing during this extended retreat.

Visit **religion.sadlierconnect.com** for more resources to extend your retreats.

Table Blessing

Bless us and this food of our retreat.
As we gather at the table,
may we appreciate and celebrate
the gift of Jesus Christ, the Son of God,
and imitate his example of loving service.
Amen.

35

Digital Resources to Extend Your Retreat

Presentations and handouts extend retreats for up to two hours!

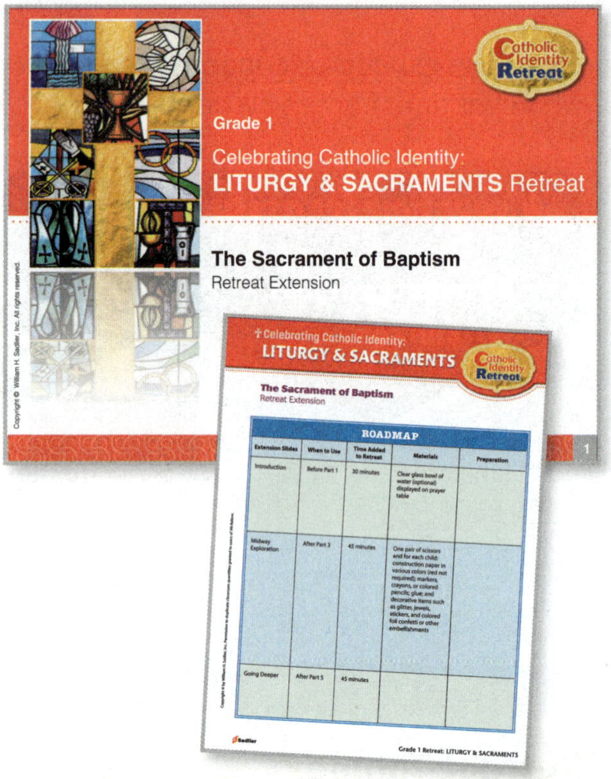

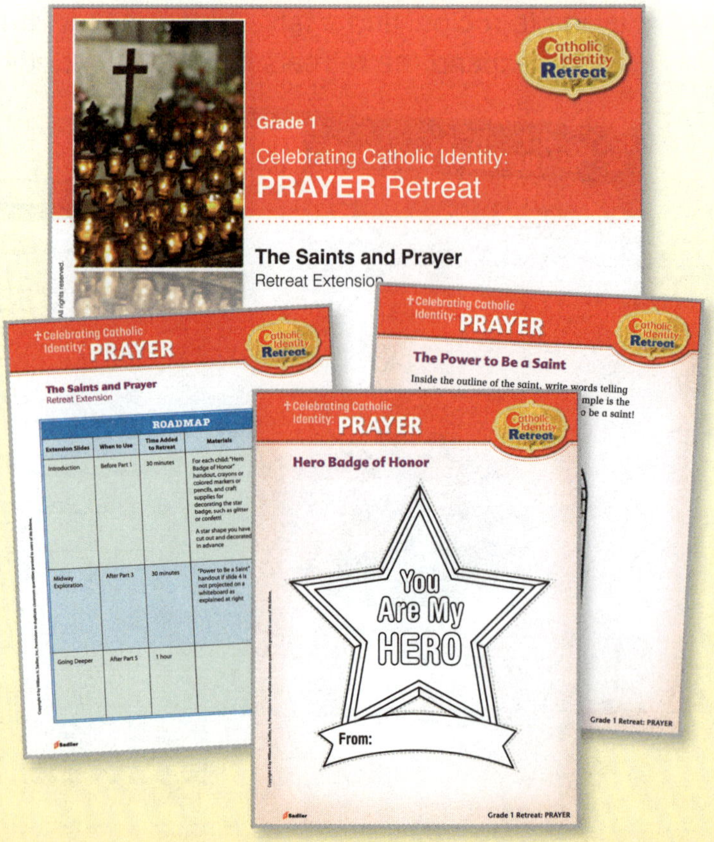

Access Your Digital Resources

Get Started

1. Go to religion.sadlierconnect.com

2. Log in

Don't have a username and password? Self register! Catechists and teachers, click "Get Started!" in the Catechist & Teacher Registration section.

3. Register a Product to gain access to program materials.

4. Select your program to begin accessing content. With one username and password, you now have access to all your Sadlier digital products.

Spirituality and Your Students

This year you will complete four *Catholic Identity Retreats* with the children on the themes of **CREED**, **LITURGY & SACRAMENTS**, **MORALITY**, and **PRAYER**. First graders are at a unique stage in their spiritual growth. As you complete these retreats, keep these characteristics of the first-grade children in mind. You can help to customize the retreat experience for the first graders by following the Retreat Considerations.

GRADE 1

Characteristics or Milestones	Retreat Considerations
Moving easily between reality and imagination, a natural foundation for responding to the joys and mysteries of God	Bring lessons of faith alive with creativity—drawing pictures, making up stories, singing songs, acting out simple plays
Understanding through active involvement with concrete objects and experiences	Engage in tactile and sensory experiences of faith, such as seeing an altar, blessing with holy water, smelling incense and candles
Growing in ability to work cooperatively with others	Encourage group or partnering activities based in mutual respect

Celebrating Catholic Identity: CREED

Catholic Identity Retreat

Retreat Theme

Creed: Jesus Christ, the Son of God

Objectives

- Appreciate that God sent his Son, Jesus, to show us his love
- Pray to Jesus, God the Son
- Identify ways to follow Jesus each day through words and actions

Background

God the Father showed his great love for us by sending his Son to save us from sin. In the mystery of the Incarnation, the Son of God assumed our human nature so that we might share in the divine life of the Holy Trinity. Jesus "became truly man while remaining truly God" (*CCC*, 464). This is the great mystery of the faith we profess in the Creed.

Jesus' divine nature is affirmed in a powerful way at his Baptism and at the Transfiguration. On both occasions, the voice from Heaven announces God's favor for his "beloved Son." The name *Jesus*, which in Hebrew means "God saves," communicates his identity. The name was given to Mary before Jesus was born. As the *Catechism of the Catholic Church* teaches, "The name 'Jesus' signifies that the very name of God is present in the person of his Son" (*CCC*, 432).

"The name of Jesus is at the heart of Christian prayer" (*CCC*, 435). In this retreat, the children will share an experience of praying a form of the Jesus Prayer. In its traditional form, the prayer calls upon Jesus with the words "Lord Jesus Christ, Son of God, have mercy on me, a sinner" (*CCC*, 435). When prayed as a contemplative prayer, the words of this prayer are repeated as a way to unite ourselves with Christ and rest in his love. This is one of many styles of contemplative prayer. Through contemplative prayer, we seek to experience God's loving presence so that we can share that love in all that we say and do.

Materials

- Pencils, markers, crayons, or colored pencils to share
- *Optional*
  - Media player
  - Soft instrumental music for reflection in Part 4
  - Bible story books and whiteboard or flipchart for Part 5
  - "Jesus in the Morning" track from the Grade 1 *We Believe* music CD

Preparation

- Read the full Leader's Guide.
- Gather materials.
- Arrange for a retreat meeting space or rearrange your classroom to accommodate a central gathering area, a space for the group to act out responses in Part 5, and a table or desk from which to lead the retreat.
- Set up the meeting space. You may arrange your leader's table or desk with a cloth in the appropriate liturgical color, an open Bible, a cross or crucifix, and a battery-operated candle.
- Make sure the children have their Grade 1 *We Believe* books on hand.

Part 1

- Tell children that this year they will learn about Jesus, the Son of God, who became one of us. Encourage the children to tell you something they already know about Jesus. Remind them of the story of Jesus' birth.
- Read the text.
- Complete the activity.
- Have children tell the stories they imagined about visiting Jesus.

Part 2

- Gather the children in the central area and settle them for prayer.
- Start the prayer with all praying the Sign of the Cross. Say the prayer together, reading the Leader parts and leading the children to pray the parts marked "All."
- Invite the children to pray quietly to Jesus using their own words as they sign the note to Jesus.
- Complete the prayer with all responding "Amen."

✝ Celebrating Catholic Identity: **CREED**

Catholic Identity Retreat

Jesus Christ, the Son of God

Part 1 **I Open My Heart**

God the Father wanted to show his love for all people. So he sent his Son, Jesus, to show his love. Jesus is the Son of God.

Jesus was born in a stable in Bethlehem.

Imagine that you visited the baby Jesus. What would you say and do? Add yourself to the picture. Then share what you imagined saying and doing when you visited Jesus.

Grade 1 Retreat: CREED R1

✝ Celebrating Catholic Identity: **CREED**

Catholic Identity Retreat

Jesus Christ, the Son of God

Part 2 **We Come Together for Prayer**

Leader: Repeat after me as we pray:
Jesus, you are the Son of God. We love you.

All: Jesus, you are the Son of God. We love you.

Leader: Jesus, you are our Lord. We honor you.

All: Jesus, you are our Lord. We honor you.

Leader: Jesus, you show us God the Father's love.
We praise you.

All: Jesus, you show us God the Father's love.
We praise you.

Leader: Sign your name to the note to Jesus.

Jesus, I love you.

Jesus is the Son of God the Father. Jesus taught that God is our Father, too. Let us love God as Jesus taught us.

All: Amen.

R2 Grade 1 Retreat: CREED

† Celebrating Catholic Identity: **CREED**

Catholic Identity Retreat

Jesus Christ, the Son of God

Part 3 I Cherish God's Word

"From the cloud came a voice that said, 'This is my beloved Son . . . listen to him.'" (Matthew 17:5)

LISTEN to the reading from Scripture. Pay close attention to the reading.

REFLECT on what you heard. Think about:

- What God said.
- How can you listen to Jesus?

SHARE your thoughts and feelings with God in prayer. Speak to God as a friend.

CONTEMPLATE or sit quietly and think about God's Word in the Scripture passage from the Gospel of Matthew above.

Grade 1 Retreat: CREED R3

† Celebrating Catholic Identity: **CREED**

Catholic Identity Retreat

Jesus Christ, the Son of God

Part 4 I Value My Catholic Faith

When we pray, we can use our own words. We can also pray without words. We can sit quietly and think about how close we are to Jesus.

We honor Jesus when we pray. We can pray:
Jesus Christ, Son of God, be with us.
(Based on the Jesus Prayer)

Make a prayer card for this Jesus Prayer. Trace the words. Draw a picture of Jesus or a symbol that makes you think of him. Remember Jesus loves you.

Share your prayer cards.

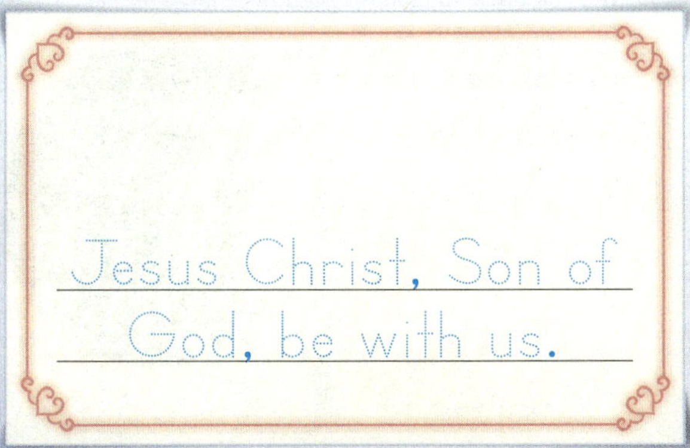

R4 Grade 1 Retreat: CREED

Part 3

- Have the children return to their individual places. Explain that they will spend some time listening to and thinking about Scripture.
- Draw attention to the image on the page. Read aloud the Scripture passage for the group.
- Read aloud each step, allowing time for the children to complete the step.
- Have volunteers share their answers to the question *How can you listen to Jesus?*

Part 4

- Explain that we honor Jesus when we pray. Explain that there are many ways to pray. Read aloud the text. Tell children that the prayer on the page comes from a special prayer called the Jesus Prayer.
- Invite the children to design the prayer card, tracing the words and drawing a picture of Jesus or a symbol that reminds them of him (such as a heart or a cross). You might play soft instrumental music for reflection as children work.
- When the children have finished their prayer cards, tell them that they will use them as you pray this Jesus Prayer together.
- Read aloud the words of the prayer three times, pausing for quiet reflection after each reading. You might have children move into different positions for each of the times you pray these words—for example, sitting, standing, and moving in a circle. During the quiet time, ask the children to look at their prayer cards and remember that Jesus loves them.

Part 5

- Read aloud the first paragraph. Name ways that Jesus shows us how to love. Preview examples from Scripture stories about Jesus featured throughout *We Believe* Grade 1 or Bible story books prepared in advance. Explain that we find stories about Jesus in the Bible.
- Have the children complete the activity. Help the children answer the questions. Loving God might be: *praying, singing, going to church*; loving ourselves might be: *resting, washing my hands, eating*; loving others might be: *sharing something, saying nice things*.
- You may wish to record responses on a whiteboard or flipchart. Arrange the children in groups, and assign one action to each group to perform.

Part 6

- Invite the children to quiet themselves once more for prayer.
- Start by praying the Sign of the Cross. Read aloud the Leader parts.
- Invite the children to join you in praying the Morning Offering by reading along with you or repeating each line after you.
- You might wish to close the prayer by singing together the "Jesus in the Morning" track from the *We Believe* Grade 1 music CD.

✝ Celebrating Catholic Identity: **CREED**

Catholic Identity Retreat

Jesus Christ, the Son of God

Part 5 I Celebrate Catholic Identity

Jesus Christ, God the Son, showed us God the Father's love. Jesus used words to show us God's love. He used actions to show us God's love. We follow Jesus when we love God, love ourselves, and love others.

Together think of an action that answers each question. Take turns acting out the answers.

How do we show that we love God?
How do we show that we love ourselves?
How do we show that we love others?

Grade 1 Retreat: CREED R5

✝ Celebrating Catholic Identity: **CREED**

Catholic Identity Retreat

Jesus Christ, the Son of God

Part 6 I Honor My Catholic Identity

(*All pray the Sign of the Cross.*)

Leader: Jesus shows us how to love. We want to follow Jesus in all we say and do. Listen to God's Word.

"Whatever you do, in word or in deed, do everything in the name of the Lord Jesus, giving thanks to God the Father through him." (Colossians 3:17)

Let us pray a special prayer. It is called the "Morning Offering." As we pray, think of one thing you can do or say today to follow Jesus.

All: My God, I offer you today
all that I think and do and say,
uniting it with what was done
on earth, by Jesus Christ,
your Son. Amen.

R6 Grade 1 Retreat: CREED

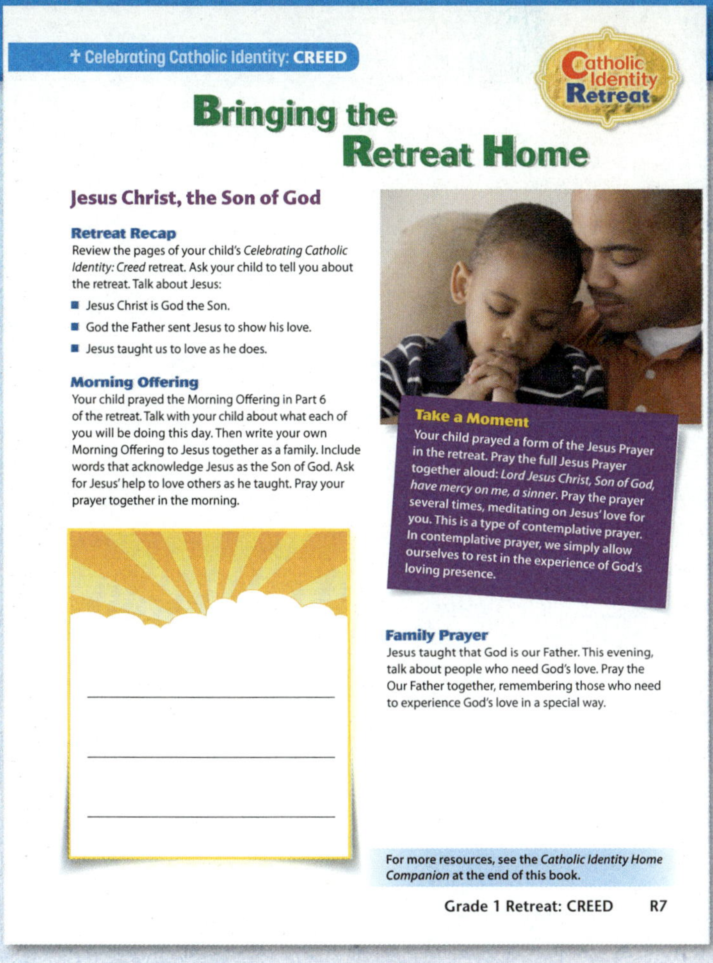

✝ Celebrating Catholic Identity: **CREED**

Catholic Identity Retreat

Bringing the Retreat Home

Jesus Christ, the Son of God

Retreat Recap

Review the pages of your child's *Celebrating Catholic Identity: Creed* retreat. Ask your child to tell you about the retreat. Talk about Jesus:

- Jesus Christ is God the Son.
- God the Father sent Jesus to show his love.
- Jesus taught us to love as he does.

Morning Offering

Your child prayed the Morning Offering in Part 6 of the retreat. Talk with your child about what each of you will be doing this day. Then write your own Morning Offering to Jesus together as a family. Include words that acknowledge Jesus as the Son of God. Ask for Jesus' help to love others as he taught. Pray your prayer together in the morning.

Take a Moment

Your child prayed a form of the Jesus Prayer in the retreat. Pray the full Jesus Prayer together aloud: *Lord Jesus Christ, Son of God, have mercy on me, a sinner.* Pray the prayer several times, meditating on Jesus' love for you. This is a type of contemplative prayer. In contemplative prayer, we simply allow ourselves to rest in the experience of God's loving presence.

Family Prayer

Jesus taught that God is our Father. This evening, talk about people who need God's love. Pray the Our Father together, remembering those who need to experience God's love in a special way.

For more resources, see the *Catholic Identity Home Companion* at the end of this book.

Grade 1 Retreat: CREED R7

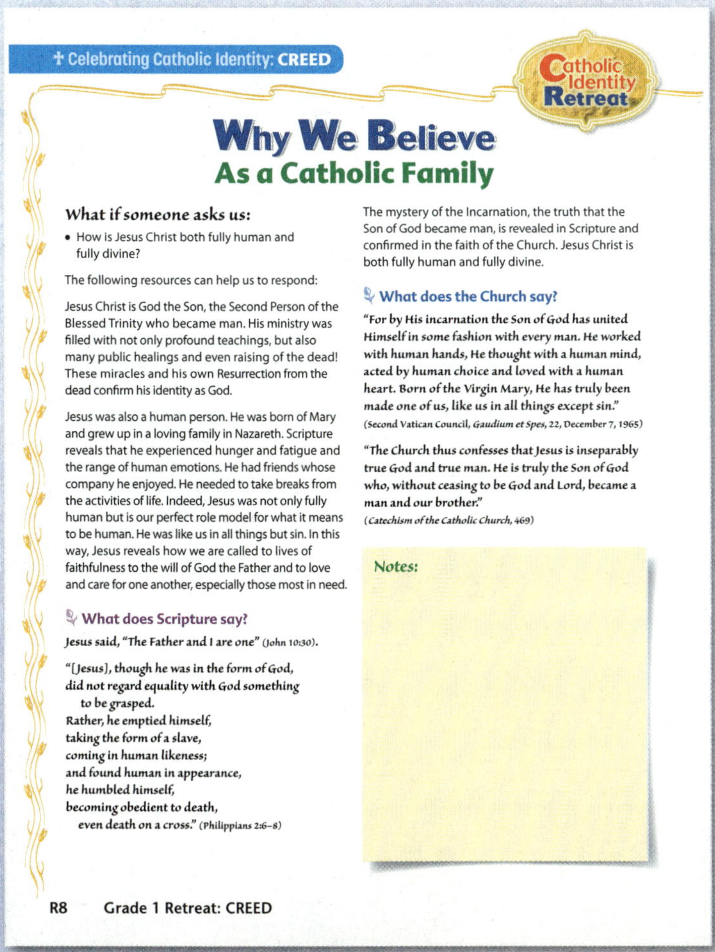

✝ Celebrating Catholic Identity: **CREED**

Catholic Identity Retreat

Why We Believe
As a Catholic Family

What if someone asks us:

- How is Jesus Christ both fully human and fully divine?

The following resources can help us to respond:

Jesus Christ is God the Son, the Second Person of the Blessed Trinity who became man. His ministry was filled with not only profound teachings, but also many public healings and even raising of the dead! These miracles and his own Resurrection from the dead confirm his identity as God.

Jesus was also a human person. He was born of Mary and grew up in a loving family in Nazareth. Scripture reveals that he experienced hunger and fatigue and the range of human emotions. He had friends whose company he enjoyed. He needed to take breaks from the activities of life. Indeed, Jesus was not only fully human but is our perfect role model for what it means to be human. He was like us in all things but sin. In this way, Jesus reveals how we are called to lives of faithfulness to the will of God the Father and to love and care for one another, especially those most in need.

What does Scripture say?

Jesus said, "The Father and I are one" (John 10:30).

"[Jesus], though he was in the form of God,
did not regard equality with God something
to be grasped.
Rather, he emptied himself,
taking the form of a slave,
coming in human likeness;
and found human in appearance,
he humbled himself,
becoming obedient to death,
even death on a cross." (Philippians 2:6–8)

The mystery of the Incarnation, the truth that the Son of God became man, is revealed in Scripture and confirmed in the faith of the Church. Jesus Christ is both fully human and fully divine.

What does the Church say?

"For by His incarnation the Son of God has united Himself in some fashion with every man. He worked with human hands, He thought with a human mind, acted by human choice and loved with a human heart. Born of the Virgin Mary, He has truly been made one of us, like us in all things except sin."
(Second Vatican Council, *Gaudium et Spes*, 22, December 7, 1965)

"The Church thus confesses that Jesus is inseparably true God and true man. He is truly the Son of God who, without ceasing to be God and Lord, became a man and our brother."
(*Catechism of the Catholic Church*, 469)

Notes:

R8 Grade 1 Retreat: CREED

Take-Home Section

Bringing the Retreat Home and *Why We Believe* together make up a special take-home section. Highlighting these family pages will help to strengthen the Catholic Identity of the family.

Encourage the children to take home *Bringing the Retreat Home* and *Why We Believe* and share them with a parent or guardian.

Bringing the Retreat Home

Invites parents to:

- live and celebrate their faith with their children.
- pray and meditate as a family.
- have their own, easy-to-do retreat at home.

◆ In the *Bringing the Retreat Home* section of the retreat on Jesus Christ, the Son of God, the family will make a Morning Offering and pray the Jesus Prayer. Invite the children to share their family's Morning Offering and describe their experience of the Jesus Prayer.

Why We Believe
As a Catholic Family

Encourages parents to:

- recall the theme of the retreat with their child.
- respond confidently to key questions about the Catholic faith relating to this theme, with a solid grounding in Scripture, Tradition, the wisdom of Catholic scholarship, the *Catechism of the Catholic Church*, and other Church documents.
- uphold their beliefs.
- evangelize others.

◆ In the *Why We Believe* section after the retreat on Jesus Christ, the Son of God, the family will find resources about the divinity and humanity of Jesus. Ask the children to tell about the resources that their family found most helpful.

Visit **religion.sadlierconnect.com** for more resources.

Notes

LITURGY & SACRAMENTS

Catholic Identity Retreat

Retreat Theme

Liturgy & Sacraments: The Sacrament of Baptism

Objectives

- Understand that Baptism makes us children of God, members of the Catholic Church, and part of the Body of Christ
- Recognize the symbols of Baptism and their significance
- Respond to the baptismal call to discipleship

Background

The word *baptize* comes from the Greek *baptizein*, meaning to "plunge" or "immerse." As we are immersed into the waters of Baptism, we die to sin and emerge as a new creation in Christ. Baptism offers all people the gift of rebirth through water and the Spirit.

The *Ephphetha* is a traditional prayer often said over the ears and mouth of an infant during the Rite of Baptism. In Baptism, infants become members of the Church, even though they cannot yet comprehend the faith. *Ephphetha* means "to open." We pray that Jesus will soon open an infant's ears to hear and and an infant's mouth to proclaim the Good News. This retreat adapts the *Ephphetha* for first graders who are beginning to understand and share their faith.

This retreat also offers the children the opportunity to engage their senses using visual and tactile elements related to the symbols of Baptism. The children will also welcome the newly baptized in their parish by making a poster.

Saint Thérèse of Lisieux embraced the idea that any action, whether big or little, when done with love, brings joy to Jesus. As a girl, Thérèse carried "sacrifice beads" or "good deed beads" that she used to count the little ways that she served God each day. The retreat offers a variation of this practice that will encourage the children to apply their baptismal calls to their own young lives. The retreat closes with a prayer based on the words of Saint Teresa of Ávila, a beloved saint and Doctor of the Church.

Materials

- Pencils, markers, crayons to share
- Symbols of Baptism: a cross, a vessel of holy water, a bowl of olive oil, a white bib, and an unlit candle
- Seven beads for each child (one of each color: brown, dark blue, light blue, yellow, white, red, orange)
- One piece of string or yarn for each child, approximately 12 inches in length, knotted on one end (1 inch from the end) and with a piece of tape affixed to the other end for easy threading of beads
- Butcher paper or large poster board
- *Optional*
  - Media player
  - Soft instrumental music
  - "Share the Light" track from the Grade 1 *We Believe* music CD

Preparation

- Read the full Leader's Guide.
- Gather materials.
- Arrange for a retreat meeting space or rearrange your classroom to accommodate a central gathering area, a table or desk from which to lead the retreat with a display of symbols of Baptism (see Materials above), and an area for activities.
- Set up the meeting space. You may arrange your leader's table or desk with a cloth in the appropriate liturgical color, an open Bible, and a battery-operated candle.
- Assign readers for Parts 2 and 6.
- Make sure the children have their Grade 1 *We Believe* books on hand.

Part 1

- Read aloud the first paragraph. If needed, offer examples such as swimming in a pool, running through a sprinkler, fishing at a lake, or splashing in the ocean.
- Ask the children to design a postcard to describe this experience, using pictures for the front and words for the back.
- Allow the children to share their postcards.
- Read aloud the paragraph below the postcard.
- Ask the children if they have seen pictures or heard stories about the day of their Baptism. Remind the children that in the waters of Baptism, we became God's children. We became brothers and sisters of Jesus. We became part of the Catholic Church, guided by the Holy Spirit.

Part 2

- Gather the children in the central area and settle them for prayer. You may wish to play meditative music or guide the children in taking a few slow, deep breaths.
- Remind the children that we were baptized in the name of the Father and of the Son and of the Holy Spirit. Water has a special role in Baptism; so does the cross. The cross reminds us of Jesus' love for us. Explain that during the prayer, we will trace the sign of the cross with our thumbs on our foreheads, ears, and mouths. Demonstrate.
- Start by praying the Sign of the Cross. Read the Leader parts and have your chosen readers read their parts. Help the children with the actions. End the prayer together.

✝ Celebrating Catholic Identity:
LITURGY & SACRAMENTS

Catholic Identity Retreat

The Sacrament of Baptism

Part 1 I Open My Heart

Have you ever spent a day by the water? Make a postcard below. Use pictures and words to tell what the day was like.

You once had a very special day at the waters of Baptism. Baptism is a sacrament. A sacrament is a special sign given to us by Jesus. Baptism is the first sacrament that we receive. It welcomes us into God's family.

Grade 1 Retreat: LITURGY & SACRAMENTS R9

✝ Celebrating Catholic Identity: LITURGY & SACRAMENTS

Catholic Identity Retreat

The Sacrament of Baptism

Part 2 We Come Together for Prayer

Leader: In Baptism, you became a child of God, a member of the Church, and a part of the Body of Christ. The waters of Baptism wash away sin and make us God's children.

Reader 1: "All you who are thirsty, come to the water!" (Isaiah 55:1)

Leader: Jesus, at the waters of Baptism, we became your brothers and sisters. Open our minds to think of you. (*Trace the cross on your forehead.*)

Jesus, at the waters of Baptism, we became your disciples, or followers. Open our ears to listen to you. (*Trace the cross on your ears.*)

Jesus, at the waters of Baptism, we became members of your Church. Open our mouths to speak the Good News. (*Trace the cross on your mouth.*)

Reader 2: "Baptism makes us members of the Body of Christ." (*Catechism of the Catholic Church*, 1267)

We are brothers and sisters in Christ. (*Join hands.*)

All: Jesus, make us one in you. Amen.

R10 Grade 1 Retreat: LITURGY & SACRAMENTS

Catholic Identity Retreat

The Sacrament of Baptism

Part 3 I Cherish God's Word

"This is how all will know that you are my disciples, if you have love for one another." (John 13:35)

LISTEN to the reading from Scripture. Pay close attention to the reading.

REFLECT on what you heard. Think about:

- Your Baptism makes you a disciple of Jesus.
- How can you follow Jesus?

SHARE your thoughts and feelings with God in prayer. Speak to God as a friend.

CONTEMPLATE or sit quietly and think about God's Word in the Scripture passage from the Gospel of John above.

Catholic Identity Retreat

The Sacrament of Baptism

Part 4 I Value My Catholic Faith

Symbols help us to understand the Sacrament of Baptism.

Welcome those being baptized in your parish! Make a welcome poster together. Use the symbols of Baptism in your poster.

Symbols of Baptism

The Sign of the Cross shows that we belong to Jesus.

The baptismal water washes away Original Sin and gives us new life.

The anointing with oil is a sign of the Gift of the Holy Spirit.

The flame of the candle reminds us of the Light of Jesus Christ.

The white garment reminds us of our new life in Christ.

Part 3

- Have the children return to their individual places. Explain that they will spend some time listening to and thinking about Scripture.
- Draw attention to the image on the page. Read aloud the Scripture passage for the group. Explain that these words are the words of Jesus.
- Read aloud each step, allowing time for the children to complete the step.
- Have volunteers share their answers to the question *How can you follow Jesus?*

Part 4

- Read aloud the text. Direct the children to look at the chart. Explain that it shows five special symbols used in celebrating the Sacrament of Baptism.
- Hold up the **cross**. Pass it around for all to see and touch. Explain that the cross reminds us of Jesus' love for us. Remind children that in Part 2, they traced a cross over their foreheads, ears, and mouths. At Baptism, parents and godparents trace the sign of the cross on the foreheads of the babies being baptized. Invite the children to close their eyes and consider the gift of Jesus' cross.
- Next, walk around the room with the vessel of **holy water** and allow the children to bless themselves. Explain that the Holy Spirit blesses the waters of Baptism in a special way. The priest or deacon pours the baptismal water three times over the head of the person being baptized. The waters of Baptism wash away all sin and give new life in the Holy Spirit. Again, invite the children to close their eyes and imagine God's water washing their souls and hearts clean.

Continued on page 12

Part 5

- Read aloud the text. Explain to the children that as baptized members of the Church, we are called to live and love as Jesus did. Our Baptism makes us disciples of Jesus.
- Give each child a piece of yarn or string (knotted at one end; at the other end, taped like the end of a shoelace for easy threading). Distribute seven colored beads to each child. Explain that the children will make special "good deeds" bracelets to wear as a reminder of their baptismal call.
- Ask the children to look at the colors of the beads. Explain that the brown bead is a reminder of the wood of Jesus' cross. The dark and light blue beads remind us of the waters of Baptism. The yellow bead is the color of Sacred Chrism. The white bead is a reminder of the white garment. The orange and red beads remind us of the flame on the candle and the light of Jesus' love that guides us through life.
- Demonstrate how to thread the beads onto the string. Invite the children to follow. When complete, help each child tie a second knot to the right of the last bead to secure. Tie each string into a bracelet that will fit around the wrist.
- Explain that this bracelet will be a daily reminder of Baptism. Explain that there is one bead for each day of the week. The beads will remind us to always follow Jesus and to share his love with others. Every deed when done out of love makes Jesus happy and shows others that we are Jesus' followers.

Part 6

- Quiet the children for prayer.
- Begin with the Sign of the Cross. Read the Leader parts and have your chosen readers read their parts. Direct the group to join together in praying the parts marked "All."
- You may wish to close with the "Share the Light" track from the Grade 1 *We Believe* music CD.

Catholic Identity Retreat

The Sacrament of Baptism

Part 5 I Celebrate Catholic Identity

In Baptism, you became Jesus' follower. Your good deeds bring joy to Jesus and show others that you are God's child.

Make a bracelet of beads to represent good deeds that you will do. This "good deeds beads" bracelet can remind you of your Baptism and your call to follow Jesus each day.

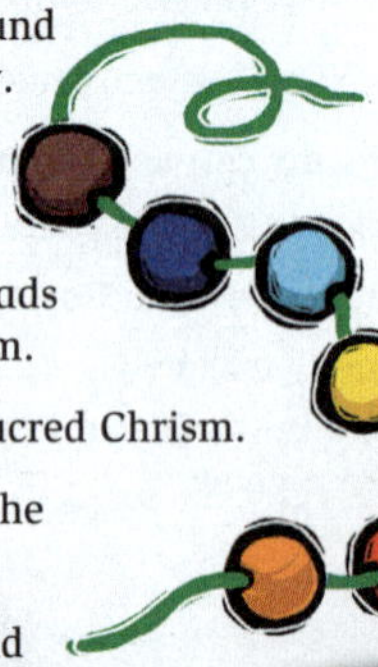

The **brown** bead is a reminder of the wood of Jesus' cross.

The **dark blue** and **light blue** beads remind us of the waters of Baptism.

The **yellow** bead is the color of Sacred Chrism.

The **white** bead is a reminder of the white garment.

The **orange** and **red** beads remind us of the flame on the candle. This light reminds us of the light of Jesus' love that guides us through life.

What good deed can you do each day? Share with your group.

Catholic Identity Retreat

The Sacrament of Baptism

Part 6 I Honor My Catholic Identity

(All pray the Sign of the Cross.)

Leader: Jesus, through Baptism, we became part of you, the Body of Christ. "Now you are Christ's body, and individually parts of it." (1 Corinthians 12:27)

Jesus, we will be your body on earth. We will live as you lived.

Reader 1: Our eyes are yours.

All: Help us to see with love and kindness.

Reader 2: Our feet are yours.

All: Help us to walk down good paths.

Reader 3: Our hands are yours.

All: Help us to bless others with our good deeds.

Leader: Jesus, we are yours.

All: Amen.

(Adapted from a prayer by Saint Teresa of Ávila)

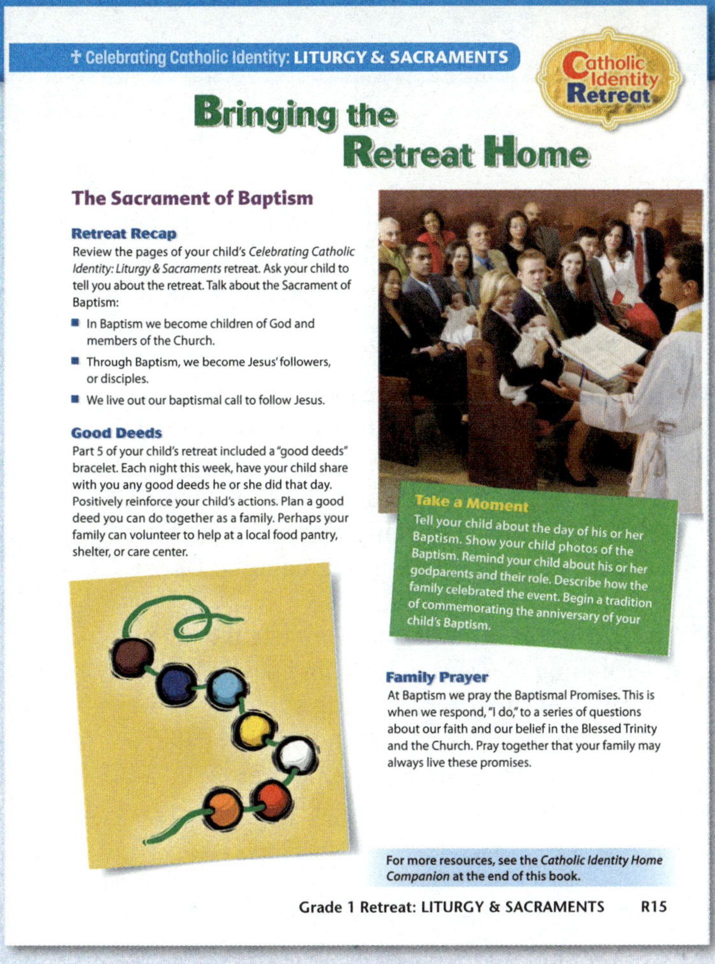

✝ Celebrating Catholic Identity: LITURGY & SACRAMENTS

Catholic Identity Retreat

Bringing the Retreat Home

The Sacrament of Baptism

Retreat Recap

Review the pages of your child's *Celebrating Catholic Identity: Liturgy & Sacraments* retreat. Ask your child to tell you about the retreat. Talk about the Sacrament of Baptism:

- In Baptism we become children of God and members of the Church.
- Through Baptism, we become Jesus' followers, or disciples.
- We live out our baptismal call to follow Jesus.

Good Deeds

Part 5 of your child's retreat included a "good deeds" bracelet. Each night this week, have your child share with you any good deeds he or she did that day. Positively reinforce your child's actions. Plan a good deed you can do together as a family. Perhaps your family can volunteer to help at a local food pantry, shelter, or care center.

Take a Moment

Tell your child about the day of his or her Baptism. Show your child photos of the Baptism. Remind your child about his or her godparents and their role. Describe how the family celebrated the event. Begin a tradition of commemorating the anniversary of your child's Baptism.

Family Prayer

At Baptism we pray the Baptismal Promises. This is when we respond, "I do," to a series of questions about our faith and our belief in the Blessed Trinity and the Church. Pray together that your family may always live these promises.

For more resources, see the *Catholic Identity Home Companion* at the end of this book.

Grade 1 Retreat: LITURGY & SACRAMENTS R15

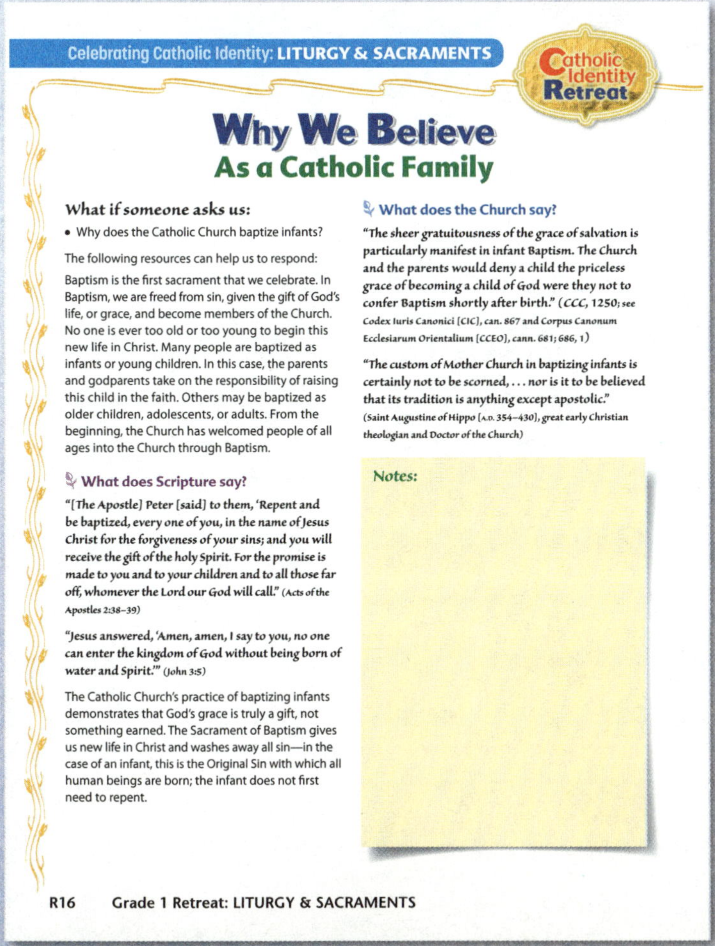

Celebrating Catholic Identity: LITURGY & SACRAMENTS

Catholic Identity Retreat

Why We Believe
As a Catholic Family

What if someone asks us:

- Why does the Catholic Church baptize infants?

The following resources can help us to respond:

Baptism is the first sacrament that we celebrate. In Baptism, we are freed from sin, given the gift of God's life, or grace, and become members of the Church. No one is ever too old or too young to begin this new life in Christ. Many people are baptized as infants or young children. In this case, the parents and godparents take on the responsibility of raising this child in the faith. Others may be baptized as older children, adolescents, or adults. From the beginning, the Church has welcomed people of all ages into the Church through Baptism.

What does Scripture say?

"[The Apostle] Peter [said] to them, 'Repent and be baptized, every one of you, in the name of Jesus Christ for the forgiveness of your sins; and you will receive the gift of the holy Spirit. For the promise is made to you and to your children and to all those far off, whomever the Lord our God will call." (Acts of the Apostles 2:38–39)

"Jesus answered, 'Amen, amen, I say to you, no one can enter the kingdom of God without being born of water and Spirit.'" (John 3:5)

The Catholic Church's practice of baptizing infants demonstrates that God's grace is truly a gift, not something earned. The Sacrament of Baptism gives us new life in Christ and washes away all sin—in the case of an infant, this is the Original Sin with which all human beings are born; the infant does not first need to repent.

What does the Church say?

"The sheer gratuitousness of the grace of salvation is particularly manifest in infant Baptism. The Church and the parents would deny a child the priceless grace of becoming a child of God were they not to confer Baptism shortly after birth." (*CCC*, 1250; see Codex Iuris Canonici [CIC], can. 867 and Corpus Canonum Ecclesiarum Orientalium [CCEO], cann. 681; 686, 1)

"The custom of Mother Church in baptizing infants is certainly not to be scorned, . . . nor is it to be believed that its tradition is anything except apostolic." (Saint Augustine of Hippo [A.D. 354–430], great early Christian theologian and Doctor of the Church)

Notes:

R16 Grade 1 Retreat: LITURGY & SACRAMENTS

Take-Home Section

Bringing the Retreat Home and *Why We Believe* together make up a special take-home section. Highlighting these family pages will help to strengthen the Catholic Identity of the family.

Encourage the children to take home *Bringing the Retreat Home* and *Why We Believe* and share them with a parent or guardian.

Bringing the Retreat Home

Invites parents to:

- live and celebrate their faith with their children.
- pray and meditate as a family.
- have their own, easy-to-do retreat at home.

◆ In the *Bringing the Retreat Home* section of the retreat on the Sacrament of Baptism, the family will plan a good deed to do together, commemorate the child's Baptism, and pray to honor their Baptismal Promises. Encourage the children to tell about the good deed their family did, perhaps sharing a photo of this event, and explain what they learned about the day of their Baptism.

Why We Believe
As a Catholic Family

Encourages parents to:

- recall the theme of the retreat with their child.
- respond confidently to key questions about the Catholic faith relating to this theme, with a solid grounding in Scripture, Tradition, the wisdom of Catholic scholarship, the *Catechism of the Catholic Church*, and other Church documents.
- uphold their beliefs.
- evangelize others.

◆ In the *Why We Believe* section after the retreat on the Sacrament of Baptism, the family will find resources about Church teaching on infant Baptism. Ask the children to tell about the resources that their family found most helpful.

Visit **religion.sadlierconnect.com** for more resources.

Continued from page 9, **Part 4**

- Pass the vessel of **oil**, allowing each child to touch the oil. (Have paper towels handy.) Explain that special oil, called Sacred Chrism, is used in Baptism. Sacred Chrism is perfumed and blessed by the bishop. Note that this oil is not Sacred Chrism, but it looks and feels the same. Explain that at Baptism, the priest or deacon traces the sign of the cross on the forehead of the person being baptized with the blessed oil, anointing him or her with the Holy Spirit. Invite the children to close their eyes and imagine the seal of oil on their foreheads, marking them as Jesus' followers.

- Pass the unlit **candle**. Ask the children to describe the job a candle has. Explain that each baptized person receives a candle. The flame represents the light of Jesus. As Jesus' followers, they will never be in darkness. They will shine Jesus' light to others. Ask the children to close their eyes and imagine a lit candle with its warmth and light. Imagine that the warmth and light are Jesus' love and joy.

- Finally, pass the **white garment**. Ask the children if they belong to any sports teams. Ask them to describe their team uniforms. Discuss how a uniform unites the team and shows belonging. Invite the children to think about the white garment as a sign of their belonging to Christ.

- Then direct the children to complete the activity of designing a poster to welcome newly baptized members of the Church, using symbols from Baptism in their poster. Use the butcher paper or poster board to create a poster as a group.

Notes

Celebrating Catholic Identity: MORALITY

Catholic Identity Retreat

Retreat Theme

Morality: Serving Others

Objectives

- Appreciate the example of service given to us by Jesus
- Recognize ways we can serve as Jesus taught us
- Put into action some of these ways to serve

Background

Throughout the Gospels, we encounter Christ's teaching by word and example how we are to love God by serving others. Again and again, Jesus served the needs of others: feeding the hungry, caring for the sick, offering words of love and forgiveness, and teaching about God's love. Jesus challenged his disciples to understand that greatness in the Kingdom of God is measured by following the example that he himself would give: "Whoever wishes to be great among you shall be your servant; whoever wishes to be first among you shall be your slave. Just so, the Son of Man did not come to be served but to serve and to give his life as a ransom for many" (Matthew 20:26–28).

The Church follows Jesus' example of loving service by teaching, preaching, healing, forgiving, comforting, and working for justice, all in Jesus' name. The Sacrament of Baptism initiates each of us into this life of service, giving us God's grace "to walk always as a child of the light" *(Rite of Baptism for Children)*. This Baptismal grace is renewed and strengthened in the Eucharist, which also *"commits us to the poor"* (CCC, 1397).

As disciples of Jesus, Christ works in us and through us so that we may show his love by serving others each day. In this retreat, the children learn about Blessed Teresa of Calcutta's emphasis on the value of even the smallest acts of charity. They will think of everyday ways to serve others, as well as plan to respond to the needs of the parish or community.

Materials

- Pencils and markers, crayons, or colored pencils to share
- Battery-operated votive candle
- *Optional*
  - Media player
  - Soft instrumental music for reflection in Parts 2 and 4
  - "Good Neighbors" track from the Grade 1 *We Believe* music CD

Preparation

- Read the full Leader's Guide.
- Gather materials.
- Arrange for a retreat meeting space or rearrange your classroom to accommodate the following: a central gathering area, space for role-playing, and a table or desk from which to lead the retreat.
- Set up the meeting space. You may arrange your leader's table or desk with a cloth in the appropriate liturgical color, an open Bible, a cross or crucifix, and a battery-operated candle.
- Make sure the children have their Grade 1 *We Believe* books on hand.

† Celebrating Catholic Identity: MORALITY

Part 1

- Briefly recall what children know about ways that Jesus served. Be sure the children understand that to serve others means to help and show that we care. Read aloud the first paragraph. Share answers to the question.
- Read aloud the second paragraph, and complete the activity.

Part 2

- Gather the children in the central area and settle them for prayer.
- Begin by praying the Sign of the Cross. Say the prayer together, reading the Leader parts. Direct children to join in praying the parts marked "All."
- After you ask the question marked "Leader," allow time for the children to complete the prayer. If you wish, play reflective music as the children work.
- Continue by asking volunteers to pray aloud their prayers and having the children read the closing prayer marked "All."

† Celebrating Catholic Identity: MORALITY

Serving Others

Part 1 I Open My Heart

We follow Jesus when we love and care for one another. Look at the picture. How does it show caring for others?

Think about times at school, with friends, or with your family. In what ways do you love and care for others? Role-play one of these ways.

Grade 1 Retreat: MORALITY R17

† Celebrating Catholic Identity: MORALITY

Serving Others

Part 2 We Come Together for Prayer

Leader: Listen to God's Word.

Jesus said, "As I have done for you, you should also do" (John 13:15).

Think about ways that Jesus served others.

Jesus told us to follow his example. Jesus, thank you for loving us. Help us to follow your example.

All: Jesus, you gave me  to serve like you.

Jesus, you gave me a  to speak kind words like you.

Jesus, you gave me a  to love like you.

Leader: How can you serve like Jesus? (*All complete the prayer below.*)

Jesus, I want to follow your example.

Help me to serve by: ______________________

____

All: Jesus, help us to show your love in all we do. Amen.

R18 Grade 1 Retreat: MORALITY

Serving Others

Part 3 I Cherish God's Word

Jesus said, "Whoever wishes to be great among you shall be your servant" (Matthew 20:26).

LISTEN to the reading from Scripture. Pay close attention to the reading.

REFLECT on what you heard. Think about:

- A servant is a person who serves others. Think of people who show love by serving others. What makes those who serve others "great," as Jesus says?

SHARE your thoughts and feelings with God in prayer. Speak to God as a friend.

CONTEMPLATE or sit quietly and think about God's Word in the Scripture passage from the Gospel of Matthew above.

Washing of the Feet, by John August Swanson

Serving Others

Part 4 I Value My Catholic Faith

Blessed Teresa of Calcutta followed Jesus by serving the poor. She helped people who had no homes. She opened schools for children. She cared for people who were sick. She said, "Do small things with great love." Even the little things we do each day can make a difference to others.

Draw one way you can serve others. You will share your drawings as a group.

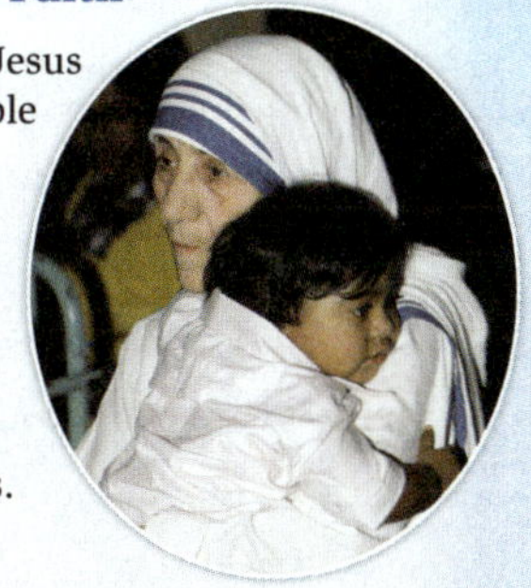

Blessed Teresa of Calcutta, holding a child, at her mission in Calcutta, India, in 1980

"Do small things with great love."

Part 3

- Have the children return to their individual places. Explain that they will spend some time listening to and thinking about Scripture.
- Draw attention to the image on the page. Read aloud the Scripture passage.
- Read aloud each step, allowing time for the children to complete the step.
- Have volunteers share their responses to the question *What makes those who serve others "great," as Jesus says?*

Part 4

- Read aloud the text.
- Ask the children to think about how even little things can make a difference. Give an example of an ordinary action that can show great love. Invite volunteers to share additional examples.
- Complete the activity. If you wish, play reflective music as the children work.
- Gather the children to share. Explain that a battery-operated candle will be lit to remind us that when our actions show love, we share the light of Christ as called to do at our Baptism.
- Teach this prayer response: "Serve the Lord with gladness."
- Light the battery-operated candle. Call children forward one at a time to describe their drawings. After each child describes his or her drawing, have the children respond, "Serve the Lord with gladness."

Part 5

- Read aloud the Scripture quotation. Point out that we can help and care for others at home, at school, and at play.
- Then explain that you will help the children plan an announcement for the parish bulletin. Discuss with the children the needs they have identified. Encourage them to suggest ways to respond to those needs. Then have the children complete the activity on the page.
- Ask the parish staff about publishing these in the bulletin. Tell the children to share their announcements at home.

Part 6

- Invite the children to quiet themselves once more for prayer.
- Begin by praying the Sign of the Cross. Say the prayer together, reading the Leader parts and leading the children to pray the responses. Then invite the children to join you in praying the Act of Love that concludes the prayer.
- You may wish to close the session by singing the "Good Neighbors" track from the Grade 1 *We Believe* music CD.

† Celebrating Catholic Identity: **MORALITY**

Serving Others

Part 5 I Celebrate Catholic Identity

"Let us not grow tired of doing good." (Galatians 6:9)

What are some of the needs that you are concerned about in your parish or community? Talk about these needs together. Then make an announcement for the parish bulletin. Ask people to be aware of these needs and to respond.

† Celebrating Catholic Identity: **MORALITY**

Serving Others

Part 6 I Honor My Catholic Identity

Leader: Jesus, help us to show your love. When we are at school,

All: help us to show your love.

Leader: When we are with our friends,

All: help us to show your love.

Leader: When we are with our families,

All: help us to show your love.

Leader: Together, let us pray an Act of Love.

All: O God, we love you above all things. Help us to love ourselves and one another as Jesus taught us to do. Amen.

Catholic Identity Retreat

Bringing the Retreat Home

Serving Others

Retreat Recap

Review the pages of your child's *Celebrating Catholic Identity: Morality* retreat. Ask your child to tell you about the retreat. Talk about serving others:

- Jesus lived a life of service.
- Jesus taught us to follow him by serving others.
- Even the little things we do each day can make a difference in others' lives.

Small Things, Great Love

Review together the saying from Part 4 of the retreat: "Do small things with great love." Make a household list of "small" everyday things your family can do for each other with great love—ordinary acts such as cleaning up, taking out garbage, making a meal, and so on—and carry these out this week.

To-Do List

☐ ____________

☐ ____________

☐ ____________

☐ ____________

☐ ____________

☐ ____________

Take a Moment

In Part 5 your child wrote an announcement about needs in the parish or community. Talk about ways your family might respond to those needs. Choose one together and make a plan to do it.

Family Prayer

Pray this together at mealtime or bedtime:

May we always give ourselves cheerfully
for the glory of your name
and the service of our neighbor,
through Christ our Lord.
(Based on the Prayer over the Offerings, Memorial of Saint Philip Neri)

For more resources, see the *Catholic Identity Home Companion* at the end of this book.

Catholic Identity Retreat

Why We Believe
As a Catholic Family

What if someone asks us:

- What is Catholic social teaching?
- Where does Catholic social teaching come from?

The following resources can help us to respond:

Jesus' entire life was one of service. Jesus' life and teaching are the foundation of Catholic social teaching. By his example and by everything he taught, Jesus upheld the dignity and rights of every human person. Human dignity is the value and worth that come from being created in God's image and likeness.

There are seven themes of Catholic social teaching:

1. Life and Dignity of the Human Person
2. Call to Family, Community, and Participation
3. Rights and Responsibilities of the Human Person
4. Option for the Poor and Vulnerable
5. Dignity of Work and the Rights of Workers
6. Solidarity of the Human Family
7. Care for God's Creation

What does Scripture say?

Jesus said, "For I was hungry and you gave me food, I was thirsty and you gave me drink, a stranger and you welcomed me, naked and you clothed me, ill and you cared for me, in prison and you visited me" (Matthew 25:35–36).

"If someone who has wordly means sees a brother in need and refuses him compassion, how can the love of God remain in him?" (1 John 3:17)

Catholic social teaching calls us to work for justice and peace as Jesus did. We are encouraged to work for change in policies and laws so that the dignity and freedom of every person may be respected.

What does the Church say?

"How can we not recognize Lazarus, the hungry beggar in the parable (cf. Lk 17:19-31), in the multitude of human beings without bread, a roof or a place to stay? How can we fail to hear Jesus: 'As you did it not to one of the least of these, you did it not to me' (Mt 25:45)?" (CCC, 2463)

"Human society . . . demands that men be guided by justice, respect the rights of others and do their duty." (Saint John XXIII, *Pacem in Terris* ("Peace on Earth"), 35)

Notes:

Take-Home Section

Bringing the Retreat Home and *Why We Believe* together make up a special take-home section. Highlighting these family pages will help to strengthen the Catholic Identity of the family.

Encourage the children to take home *Bringing the Retreat Home* and *Why We Believe* and share them with a parent or guardian.

Bringing the Retreat Home

Invites parents to:

- live and celebrate their faith with their children.
- pray and meditate as a family.
- have their own, easy-to-do retreat at home.

In the *Bringing the Retreat Home* section of the retreat on serving others, the family will list everyday things to do with great love, choose a need to address in the parish or community, and pray a family prayer about service. Invite the children to tell about an everyday way their family served and their family's plans to address a need in the parish or community.

Why We Believe
As a Catholic Family

Encourages parents to:

- recall the theme of the retreat with their child.
- respond confidently to key questions about the Catholic faith relating to this theme, with a solid grounding in Scripture, Tradition, the wisdom of Catholic scholarship, the *Catechism of the Catholic Church*, and other Church documents.
- uphold their beliefs.
- evangelize others.

In the *Why We Believe* section after the retreat on serving others, the family will find resources about Catholic social teaching. Ask the children to tell about the resources that their family found most helpful.

Visit **religion.sadlierconnect.com** for more resources.

Notes

Catholic Identity Retreat

Retreat Theme

Prayer: The Saints and Prayer

Objectives

- Understand that we are united with the saints in our worship and praise of God
- Identify ways in which the saints are examples of holiness for us
- Recognize ways to pray with the saints

Background

The Church is a Communion of Saints (*CCC*, 946). In the liturgy, we are joined with those living now on earth and also with the souls in Purgatory and the saints in Heaven. Together, with this entire Communion of Saints, we give praise to God.

Throughout the Church year, we honor the saints—holy men and women who imitated Jesus Christ. We call upon the saints for help by asking them to pray for us. The prayers and good works of the saints are a treasury that is shared with us so that we too may share the joy of Heaven.

The saints are honored as well through personal prayer and devotion. Feast days of the saints are remembered in homes and communities as times for special prayer and celebration (for example, processions in honor of Our Lady of Guadalupe and meals in honor of Saint Joseph's feast day). Devotion to the saints is also expressed through sacramentals such as relics, medals, icons, and statues, reminding us of our bond with those who have gone before us in the faith. Many saints are identified as patrons for particular causes or locations, and we ask for their prayers for these specific needs or places.

This retreat helps reinforce what the children know about saints, brings the children together to pray liturgical prayers that honor the saints, and encourages them to think about how saints would respond to situations.

Materials

- Pencils and markers, crayons, or colored pencils to share
- *Optional*
  - Media player
  - Soft instrumental music for Part 5
  - "When the Saints Go Marching In" from Grade 1 *We Believe* music CD
  - A selection of children's books about the saints and a Catholic liturgical calendar or a book of saints to identify saints' feast days (for more resources, visit **religion.sadlierconnect.com**)

Preparation

- Read the full Leader's Guide.
- Gather materials.
- Arrange for a retreat meeting space or rearrange your classroom to accommodate the following: a central gathering area and a table or desk from which to lead the retreat.
- Set up the meeting space. You may arrange your leader's table or desk with a cloth in the color of the liturgical season; an open Bible; a cross or crucifix; a battery-operated candle; and statues, icons, or holy cards of Mary and the saints.
- Assign a reader for Part 6 of the retreat.
- Make sure the children have their Grade 1 *We Believe* books on hand.

Part 1

- Read the first paragraph.
- Recall what the children have been learning about saints in their *We Believe* books.
- Complete the activity.
- Allow time for the group to share.

Part 2

- Gather the children in the central area and settle them for prayer.
- Begin by praying the Sign of the Cross. Say the prayer together, reading the Leader part and having the children pray the "All" response with the gesture indicated.

✝ Celebrating Catholic Identity: **PRAYER**

The Saints and Prayer

Part 1 I Open My Heart

What have you learned about saints? Think of one saint you have learned about. Complete the stained glass window to show this saint.

Share your stained glass saint picture. Share what you know about this saint with the group.

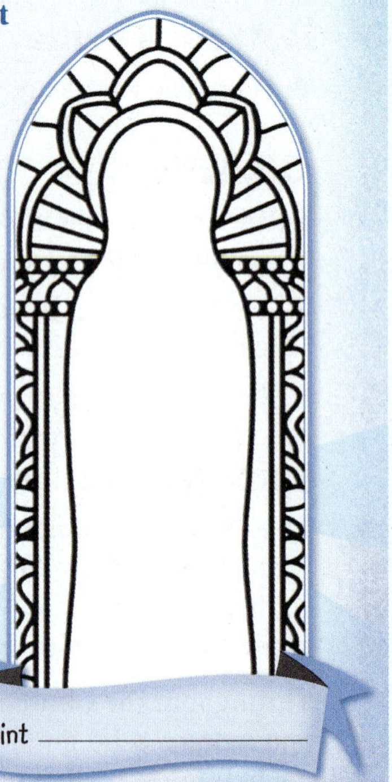

Grade 1 Retreat: PRAYER R25

✝ Celebrating Catholic Identity: **PRAYER**

The Saints and Prayer

Part 2 We Come Together for Prayer

Leader: When we pray at Mass, we worship God.

In the Mass, we praise God with the saints. The priest prays:

And so, with the Angels
and all the Saints,
we declare your glory,
as with one voice we acclaim:
(Based on Eucharistic Prayer II)

We respond:

All: (*All raise arms up, palms facing upward, as a sign of praise.*)
Holy, Holy, Holy Lord God of hosts.
Heaven and earth are full of your glory.
Hosanna in the highest.
Blessed is he who comes in the name of the Lord.
Hosanna in the highest.
Amen.

R26 Grade 1 Retreat: PRAYER

The Saints and Prayer

Part 3 I Cherish God's Word

"Be imitators of God, as beloved children, and live in love, as Christ loved us." (Ephesians 5:1–2)

LISTEN to the reading from Scripture. Pay close attention to the reading.

REFLECT on what you heard. Think about:

- How the saints loved others, as Christ did.
- How can you follow the example of the saints?

SHARE your thoughts and feelings with God in prayer. Speak to God as a friend.

CONTEMPLATE or sit quietly and think about God's Word in the Scripture passage from the Letter of Saint Paul to the Ephesians above.

Communion of Saints tapestries, by John Nava, Cathedral of Our Lady of the Angels, Los Angeles, CA

The Saints and Prayer

Part 4 I Value My Catholic Faith

Saints loved others as Christ did. The best way to honor a saint is to follow his or her example. Write what you think a saint would do.

What's happening?	What would a saint do?
There is a new student in your class.	
Someone is being bullied in the playground.	
A younger child gets hurt coming to school.	

Part 3

- Have the children return to their individual places. Explain that they will spend some time listening to and thinking about Scripture.
- Draw attention to the image on the page. Read aloud the Scripture passage.
- Read aloud each step, allowing time for the children to complete the step.
- Have volunteers share their answers to the question *How can you follow the example of the saints?*

Part 4

- Gather again in the central gathering space.
- Read aloud the text.
- Complete the activity.
- Encourage the children to share what they wrote for each situation. If there is time, have volunteers act out each situation.

Part 5

- Have the children return to their individual places. Read aloud the text.
- Again, you may wish to review saints the children have learned about in their books. Help the children recall what these saints did during their lives.
- Complete the activity. You may wish to play reflective music while the children work.
- Allow time for sharing.

Part 6

- Invite the children to quiet themselves once more for prayer.
- Begin by praying the Sign of the Cross. Say the prayer together, reading the Leader parts and having your chosen reader read his or her part.
- Remind the children that Mary is the greatest saint. She loved others as Jesus did.
- Then invite the children to bow their heads as you pray the blessing prayer from the Solemnity of All Saints. All the children should then respond, "Amen."
- You may wish to close by singing the "When the Saints Go Marching In" track from the Grade 1 *We Believe* music CD.

Catholic Identity Retreat

The Saints and Prayer

Part 5 I Celebrate Catholic Identity

Pope Francis said, "To see God, to be like God: this is our hope."
(Pope Francis, homily for Solemnity of All Saints, November 1, 2013)

The saints give us hope. We can follow their example.

You can be a saint! Work with a partner to list the things you could do in your life to follow the example of the saints. Tell about good things you have done, like the saints.

Share your list with the whole group.

Catholic Identity Retreat

The Saints and Prayer

Part 6 I Honor My Catholic Identity

Leader: Mary, the mother of Jesus, and all the other saints help us by their prayers. They pray for us that we may live forever with God as they do. Listen to God's Word.

Reader: "May the God of peace . . . make you perfectly holy."
(1 Thessalonians 5:23)

Leader: God, we praise you for the lives of the saints. Hear their prayers for us and help us to learn from their example. Bow your heads for a blessing.

May God, the glory and joy of
the Saints,
who has caused you to be strengthened
by means of their outstanding prayers,
bless you with unending blessings.

All: Amen.
(Solemn Blessing, Solemnity of All Saints)

Catholic Identity Retreat

Bringing the Retreat Home

The Saints and Prayer

Retreat Recap

Review the pages of your child's *Celebrating Catholic Identity: Prayer* retreat. Ask your child to tell you about the retreat. Talk about the saints and prayer:

- Saints are followers of Jesus who loved him very much.
- We honor the saints throughout the year and are united with the saints when we pray at Mass.
- The saints pray for us.

Patron Saint of the Family

"Dedicate" your family to a patron saint. Together choose a saint that has particular meaning for your family. Compose a family prayer in honor of this saint. You may wish to display an image of this saint in the home.

Saint ____________________

Take a Moment

Many prayers by or in honor of the saints have become an important part of our Catholic tradition. Think of one of these prayers that you know, and pray it aloud together. For example, the Hail Mary honors our greatest saint, Mary, the Mother of God. You may wish to review the *Prayers and Practices* or *Catholic Identity Home Companion* at the end of your child's book for further ideas.

Family Prayer

A litany is a prayer made up of short titles for God, Jesus, Mary, or other saints or holy people. After each title, we pray a short response, such as "Hear our prayer" or "Pray for us." Pray together a litany using the names of saints. You may wish to review your child's Chapter 25 for saints to include.

For more resources, see the *Catholic Identity Home Companion* at the end of this book.

Catholic Identity Retreat

Why We Believe
As a Catholic Family

What if someone asks us:

- Why do Catholics have devotions to saints?

The following resources can help us to respond:

Devotions are expressions of prayer that are handed down through the centuries. Many devotions honor Mary, and other devotions honor a particular saint or group of saints. Saints are our fellow Christians who are now with God in Heaven and whose holy lives have taught us the way of discipleship.

When we pray to the saints, we are really asking the saints to pray to God for us—to *intercede* for us. The practice of asking the saints for help in living the Christian life dates to the earliest days of the Church.

What does Scripture say?

"We are surrounded by so great a cloud of witnesses. . . ."; ". . . the assembly of the firstborn enrolled in heaven, and God the judge of all, and the spirits of the just made perfect." (Hebrews 12:1, 23)

"I kneel before the Father, from whom every family in heaven and on earth is named." (Ephesians 3:14–15)

All grace and power come from God. But God grants special gifts to the saints to help us as we are still journeying to Heaven. We ask for their blessing; we ask them to join with us in our prayer before God. As Catholics we can be in relationship with saints, with all in Heaven. It is a beautiful element of Catholic faith that we should celebrate. It is called the Communion of Saints.

Perhaps you have encountered questions about our practice of asking the saints to pray for us. Millions of Christians have lived before us, and because of their holy lives, the Church honors them and calls them saints. Any person in Heaven is a saint. Over the history of Christianity, the Church has given the official title of "Saint" to people known to have led particularly remarkable lives of holiness and who have had verifiable miracles occur through their intercession.

What does the Church say?

"By keeping the memorials of the saints—first of all the holy Mother of God, then the apostles, the martyrs, and other saints—on fixed days of the liturgical year, the Church on earth shows that she is united with the liturgy of heaven. She gives glory to Christ for having accomplished his salvation in his glorified members; their example encourages her on her way to the Father." (*CCC*, 1195)

"What is the Church if not the assembly of all the saints?" (Saint Nicetas, one of the Church Fathers, A.D. 334–414, as quoted in *CCC*, 946)

"Do not weep, for I shall be more useful to you after my death, and I shall help you then more effectively than during my life." (Saint Dominic, founder of the Dominicans, about 1170–1221, as quoted in *CCC*, 956)

Notes:

Take-Home Section

Bringing the Retreat Home and *Why We Believe* together make up a special take-home section. Highlighting these family pages will help to strengthen the Catholic Identity of the family.

Encourage the children to take home *Bringing the Retreat Home* and *Why We Believe* and share them with a parent or guardian.

Bringing the Retreat Home

Invites parents to:

- live and celebrate their faith with their children.
- pray and meditate as a family.
- have their own, easy-to-do retreat at home.

In the *Bringing the Retreat Home* section of the retreat on the saints and prayer, the family will dedicate the family to a patron saint, pray together a prayer by or in honor of a saint, and pray a litany of the saints. Invite the children to tell about their family's patron saint and share the prayers the family chose to pray together.

Why We Believe
As a Catholic Family

Encourages parents to:

- recall the theme of the retreat with their child.
- respond confidently to key questions about the Catholic faith relating to this theme, with a solid grounding in Scripture, Tradition, the wisdom of Catholic scholarship, the *Catechism of the Catholic Church*, and other Church documents.
- uphold their beliefs.
- evangelize others.

In the *Why We Believe* section after the retreat on the saints and prayer, the family will find resources about why Catholics have devotions to saints. Ask the children to tell about the resources that their family found most helpful.

Visit **religion.sadlierconnect.com** for more resources.

Notes

Catholic Identity Q&A

In this section, you will find questions and answers that review the content in your *We Believe: Catholic Identity Edition* book this year. Each question in this section covers the key Catholic teachings in your book, in chapter order. Answer each question to review what you have learned—whether you use this section at home, in school, or in the parish. The answers provided will strengthen your understanding of your Catholic faith and help to reinforce your Catholic Identity.

The *CCC* references after each answer indicate where to find further information about that answer in the *Catechism of the Catholic Church.*

Q: Why did God create us?

A: God created us to know, love, and serve him. CCC, 356, 357, 358

Q: What is the Blessed Trinity?

A: The Blessed Trinity is One God in Three Persons: God the Father, God the Son, and God the Holy Spirit. CCC, 254

Q: What is prayer?

A: Prayer is listening to and talking to God. CCC, 2559

CCC = Catechism of the Catholic Church

Parish page 257 / School page 337

Q: What is the Holy Family?

A: The Holy Family is Jesus, Mary, and Joseph. CCC, 533, 1655

Q: How did Jesus share God's love with all people?

A: Jesus went from town to town teaching people about God. He treated all people with respect. He shared the news of God's love with everyone. CCC, 544, 561

Q: What are commandments?

A: Commandments are laws given to us by God. CCC, 2056–2058

Q: How do we follow the Great Commandment that Jesus gave us?

A: We follow the Great Commandment when we love God, ourselves, and others. CCC, 2055

Q: What do we do throughout the Church year?

A: All year long the Church gathers to thank God for his great love. Together, we praise God. We celebrate all that Jesus did for us. CCC, 1168, 1171, 1172

Parish page 258 / School page 338

Catholic Identity Q&A

The *Catholic Identity Q&A* section reviews and reinforces grade-level doctrine to strengthen Catholic Identity. Each question in this section covers key Catholic teachings in the student book in the order in which they were taught.

At the end of each answer you will find the relevant paragraph number(s) from the *Catechism of the Catholic Church* for further reading and enrichment.

Catholic Identity Q&A

Children may use the *Catholic Identity Q&A* pages to review what they have learned in this year's program. You can use these questions and answers with the children to prepare for an assessment. You may have the children practice the questions and answers in class or at home with their families.

Q: What do we celebrate during Ordinary Time?

A: During Ordinary Time we celebrate Jesus' life and teachings. CCC, 1163, 1168, 1172, 1173, 1195

Q: Who are the Apostles?

A: The Apostles were the twelve men Jesus chose to lead his followers. CCC, 858

Q: What prayer did Jesus teach his followers?

A: Jesus taught his followers the Lord's Prayer. We also call this prayer the Our Father. CCC, 2759, 2761

Q: What is Pentecost?

A: Pentecost is the day the Holy Spirit came to Jesus' followers. CCC, 1076

Q: What is the Church?

A: The Church is all the people who are baptized in Jesus and follow his teachings. CCC, 752, 759

Q: Who leads and cares for the Church?

A: The pope and bishops lead and care for the whole Church. CCC, 861, 862, 869

Parish page 259 / School page 339

Q: What is Advent?

A: Advent is a special time when we get ready for the coming of God's Son, Jesus. CCC, 524

Q: What do we celebrate at Christmas?

A: At Christmas we celebrate the birth of the Son of God, Jesus. CCC, 1171

Q: What is a parish?

A: A parish is a group of Catholics who join together to share God's love. CCC, 2179

Q: What is a sacrament?

A: A sacrament is a special sign given to us by Jesus that gives us his love. CCC, 1131

Q: What is Baptism?

A: Baptism is the sacrament in which we become children of God and members of the Church. CCC, 1213

Q: What is grace?

A: Grace is God's life in us. CCC, 1997

Parish page 260 / School page 340

Q: What happens when we celebrate the Sacrament of Penance and Reconciliation?

A: When we celebrate the Sacrament of Penance and Reconciliation, we receive and celebrate God's forgiveness. CCC, 1422, 1440

Q: What is Lent?

A: Lent is a special time to get ready for the Church's celebration of Jesus' Resurrection. CCC, 1438

Q: What is the Eucharist?

A: The Eucharist is the sacrament in which, by the power of the Holy Spirit, the bread and wine become the Body and Blood of Jesus Christ. CCC, 1323, 1413

Q: What is the Mass?

A: The Mass is the celebration of the Eucharist. CCC, 1382

Q: What do we do at Mass?

A: At Mass we gather to worship God. We listen to God's Word. Our gifts of bread and wine become the Body and Blood of Christ, which are received in Holy Communion. CCC, 1346, 1348, 1355

Parish page 261 / School page 341

Q: What is the Gospel?

A: The Gospel is the Good News about Jesus Christ and his teachings. CCC, 125

Q: Why do we honor Mary and the saints?

A: The Church honors Mary because she is the Mother of Jesus, God the Son. The Church honors the saints because they are followers of Jesus who have died and now live forever with God. CCC, 828, 829, 2683

Q: How can we care for the gifts of God's creation?

A: God wants us to use our gifts and talents to care for all people. He also wants us to care for all creation. CCC, 299, 2415

Q: What do we celebrate during Easter?

A: During Easter we celebrate that Jesus Christ rose from the dead. CCC, 1169

Parish page 262 / School page 342

Catholic Identity Q&A

The content of the *Catholic Identity Q&A* can be formatted for use as flash cards, crossword puzzles, games, etc., to provide alternative review and practice.

Resources for the Family

The *Catholic Identity Home Companion* is a treasury of Catholic prayers, practices, and devotions for strengthening Catholic Identity in the school, parish, home, and community. The content is organized by the four pillars of the *Catechism of the Catholic Church*.

This section has been designed to help immerse children and their families in additional resources related to the four themes of the retreats in the student book: **CREED**, **LITURGY & SACRAMENTS**, **MORALITY**, and **PRAYER**. The family is encouraged to visit this section at the end of the take-home page, *Bringing the Retreat Home*, following each *Celebrating Catholic Identity* retreat in the student book.

For each theme, the children and their families will find prayers, practices, devotions, traditions, and other aspects of Catholic spirituality and beliefs to share and incorporate into their lives as a Catholic family. Encourage the children to visit this section with their families when they complete *Bringing the Retreat Home*. The family might also share this section independently of the retreats, as part of a family catechesis program or during a family gathering.

Spirituality and Your First-Grade Child

This section helps to introduce the family to some of the commonalities of spiritual development among children at this grade level. It also offers ways the family can build upon the spiritual growth of the child. Invite the children to share this page at home and to talk with the family about ways they might grow in spirituality based on any of the recommendations provided.

Catholic Identity Home Companion

Resources for the Family

In this section, you will find a treasury of resources to help build up your Catholic Identity at home, in your parish, and in the community. Learn more about key Catholic teachings from the themes of your child's *Celebrating Catholic Identity* retreats: **CREED**, **LITURGY & SACRAMENTS**, **MORALITY**, and **PRAYER**. For each theme, you will find Catholic prayers, practices, and devotions to share with those you love—and make a part of your daily lives as a Catholic family!

Family: "the place where parents pass on the faith to their children."
—Pope Francis
Apostolic Exhortation *Evangelii Gaudium*, 66

Parish page 263 / School page 343

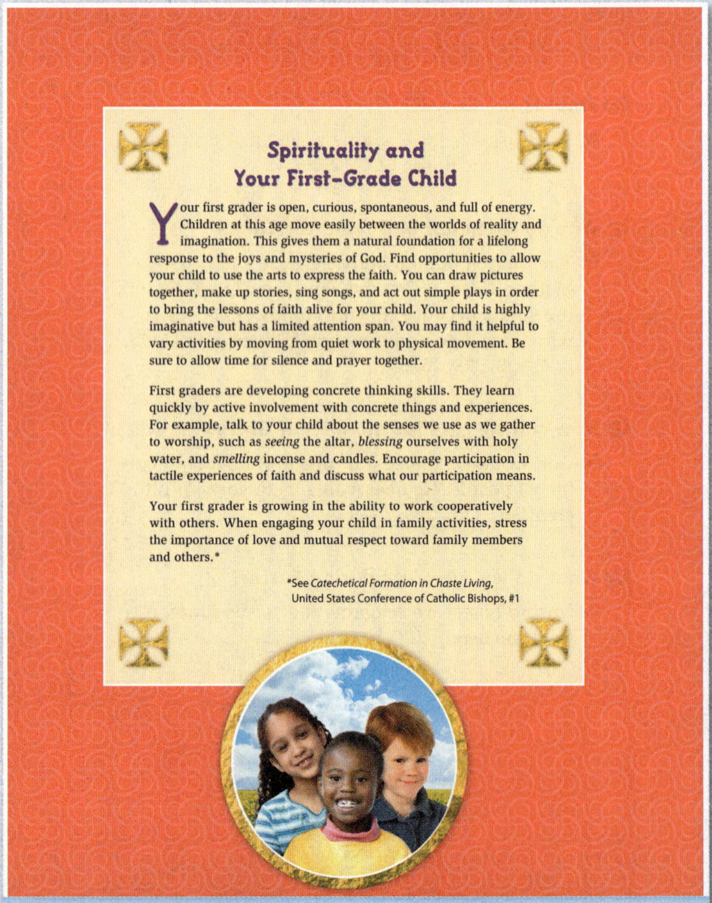

Spirituality and Your First-Grade Child

Your first grader is open, curious, spontaneous, and full of energy. Children at this age move easily between the worlds of reality and imagination. This gives them a natural foundation for a lifelong response to the joys and mysteries of God. Find opportunities to allow your child to use the arts to express the faith. You can draw pictures together, make up stories, sing songs, and act out simple plays in order to bring the lessons of faith alive for your child. Your child is highly imaginative but has a limited attention span. You may find it helpful to vary activities by moving from quiet work to physical movement. Be sure to allow time for silence and prayer together.

First graders are developing concrete thinking skills. They learn quickly by active involvement with concrete things and experiences. For example, talk to your child about the senses we use as we gather to worship, such as *seeing* the altar, *blessing* ourselves with holy water, and *smelling* incense and candles. Encourage participation in tactile experiences of faith and discuss what our participation means.

Your first grader is growing in the ability to work cooperatively with others. When engaging your child in family activities, stress the importance of love and mutual respect toward family members and others.*

*See *Catechetical Formation in Chaste Living*, United States Conference of Catholic Bishops, #1

Parish page 264 / School page 344

CREED

Jesus Christ, the Son of God

Jesus is God the Son who became one of us. He grew up in a family. Jesus prayed every morning and every night with his mother, Mary, and his foster father, Joseph. Jesus' family showed their love for God and one another.

In the Nicene Creed, we express our belief in Jesus. Explain to your child that the Nicene Creed is the creed we often pray at Mass on Sunday. Pray the Creed together and note the parts that refer to Jesus.

Nicene Creed

I believe in one God,
the Father almighty,
maker of heaven and earth,
of all things visible and invisible.

I believe in one Lord Jesus Christ,
the Only Begotten Son of God,
born of the Father before all ages.
God from God, Light from Light,
true God from true God,
begotten, not made, consubstantial
with the Father;
through him all things were made.
For us men and for our salvation
he came down from heaven,
and by the Holy Spirit
was incarnate of the Virgin Mary,
and became man.

For our sake he was crucified
under Pontius Pilate,
he suffered death and was buried,
and rose again on the third day
in accordance with the Scriptures.
He ascended into heaven
and is seated at the right hand
of the Father.
He will come again in glory to judge
the living and the dead
and his kingdom will have no end.

I believe in the Holy Spirit, the Lord,
the giver of life,
who proceeds from the Father and the Son,
who with the Father and the Son is
adored and glorified,
who has spoken through the prophets.

I believe in one, holy, catholic
and apostolic Church.
I confess one Baptism for the
forgiveness of sins
and I look forward to the resurrection of the
dead and the life of the world to come.
Amen.

CREED

119 Luke, 10 — Book, Chapter

Passage Title — Praise of the Father
Titles are sometimes added to show themes of the chapters, but these titles are not part of the actual words of the Bible.

Verse — 21

Passage — 21 t u*At that very moment he rejoiced [in] the holy Spirit and said, "I give you praise, Father, Lord of heaven and earth, for although you have hidden these things from the wise and the learned you have revealed them to the childlike. Yes, Father, such has been your gracious will. 22 vAll things have been handed over to me by my Father. No one knows who the Son is except the Father, and who the Father is except the Son and anyone to whom the Son wishes to reveal him."
A passage is a section of a chapter made up of a number of verses.

This passage shows Luke 10:21–22, which means: the Gospel of Luke, chapter ten, verses twenty-one to twenty-two.

Reading the Bible . . . in Five Easy Steps

When you are given a Scripture passage to read, here are five easy steps that will help you to find it! With your child, follow these steps to look up **Lk 10:21–22**.

1. **Find the book.** When the name of the book is abbreviated, locate the meaning of the abbreviation on the contents pages at the beginning of your Bible. *Lk* stands for Luke, one of the four Gospels.
2. **Find the page.** Your Bible's contents pages will also show the page on which the book begins. Turn to that page within your Bible.
3. **Find the chapter.** Once you arrive at the page where the book begins, keep turning the pages forward until you find the right chapter. The image above shows you how a chapter number is usually displayed on a typical Bible page. You are looking for chapter **10** in Luke.
4. **Find the verses.** Once you find the right chapter, locate the verse or verses you need within the chapter. The image above also shows you how verse numbers will look on a typical Bible page. You are looking for verses **21** and **22**.
5. **Start reading!**

CREED

Jesus Christ, the Son of God

Encourage the children to share this section at home. Suggest that they introduce the section by reminding their families that Jesus Christ is the Son of God, the Second Person of the Blessed Trinity.

Nicene Creed

To prepare the children to share this prayer with their families, explain that a *creed* is a statement of our beliefs. Point out that we profess the Nicene Creed every Sunday at Mass.

Recommend that the children pray aloud the Nicene Creed with their families. As they identify at home the words from the Nicene Creed that refer to Jesus, encourage children to indicate these words by underlining them. Invite the children to share what they underlined at the next class session.

Reading the Bible . . . in Five Easy Steps

To prepare the children to share this section at home, demonstrate in class the steps for looking up a Scripture passage as described on the page. Also invite the children to make sure the family has a Bible they can use to actually complete the steps at home with their families. (You might send home a Bible or have the children check in advance for a Bible at home that may be used.)

LITURGY & SACRAMENTS

The Power of Grace

Prepare the children to share this section at home by reminding them that grace is our share in God's life and love, and we receive grace in the sacraments.

A Virtuous Life

Explain that faith, hope, and love (or charity) are the theological virtues. We receive these virtues at Baptism. You may want a volunteer to read Saint Paul's words about these virtues in 1 Corinthians Chapter 13. For each of the Acts of Faith, Hope, and Love provided in this section, you might have the children practice the prayer aloud before sharing it with their families so that they can lead the family in praying at home.

Holy Days of Obligation

Explain that the Holy Days of Obligation are certain days during the liturgical year when we celebrate the special events of Jesus' life and the honors given to Mary. Point out that Catholics are obliged to participate in the Mass on these days. You might suggest that the children work with their families to make a card to display the Holy Days of Obligation as a reminder for everyone in the family.

LITURGY & SACRAMENTS

The Power of Grace

How do we live as disciples of Jesus? Through the power of God's grace, we can grow in our friendship with God. Grace is a share in God's life and love. We receive grace at our Baptism and when we receive the other sacraments. The water of Baptism is a sign of the life that God gives us through his grace. Throughout our lives, grace helps us respond to God with love. It gives us the strength to live as Jesus' disciples.

A Virtuous Life

A virtue is a good habit that helps us to act according to God's plan for us. Virtues help guide our conduct with the help of God's grace. The virtues of faith, hope, and charity are theological virtues. These virtues are called theological virtues because they are gifts from God.

An Act of Faith
O God, we believe in all that Jesus has taught us about you.
We place all our trust in you because of your great love for us.

An Act of Hope
O God, we never give up on your love. We have hope and will work for your kingdom to come and for a life that lasts forever with you in heaven.

An Act of Love
O God, we love you above all things. Help us to love ourselves and one another as Jesus taught us to do.

Parish page 267 / School page 347

LITURGY & SACRAMENTS

Holy Days of Obligation

The liturgy is the official public prayer of the Church. In the liturgy we gather as a community joined to Christ to celebrate what we believe. The Church year is based on the life of Christ and the celebration of his life in the liturgy. The Church's year is called the liturgical year. In one liturgical year we recall and celebrate the whole life of Jesus Christ. We also honor Mary and the saints, who show us how to live as disciples of Jesus.

Each Sunday of the liturgical year is a great celebration of the Church, or a solemnity. In addition to each Sunday, there are other solemnities in the liturgical year on which we are obliged to attend Mass to give special honor to Jesus Christ for the salvation he has given to us. These are called holy days of obligation.

Holy days of obligation celebrated by the Church in the United States:

- Solemnity of Mary, Mother of God (January 1)
- Ascension (when celebrated on Thursday during the Easter season*)
- Assumption of Mary (August 15)
- All Saints' Day (November 1)
- Immaculate Conception (December 8)
- Christmas (December 25)

**Some dioceses celebrate the Ascension on the following Sunday.*

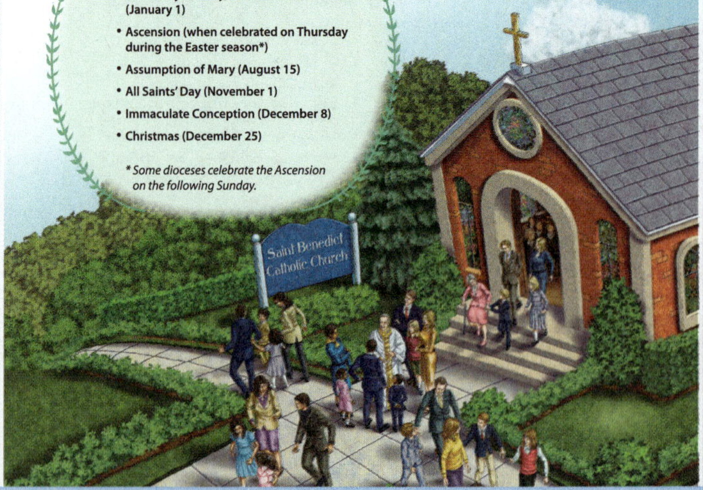

Parish page 268 / School page 348

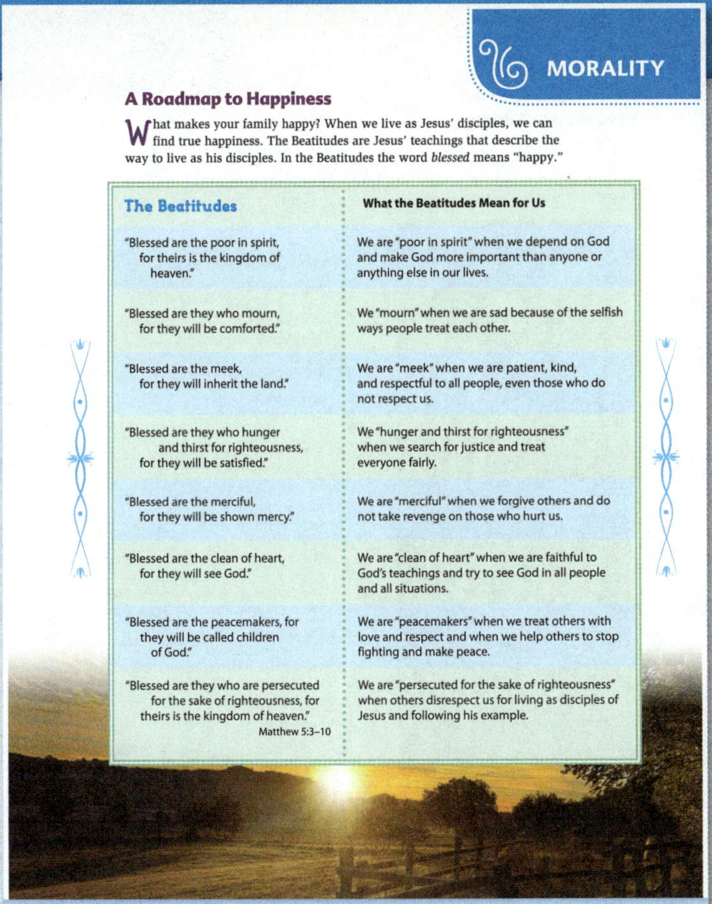

MORALITY

A Roadmap to Happiness

What makes your family happy? When we live as Jesus' disciples, we can find true happiness. The Beatitudes are Jesus' teachings that describe the way to live as his disciples. In the Beatitudes the word *blessed* means "happy."

The Beatitudes	What the Beatitudes Mean for Us
"Blessed are the poor in spirit, for theirs is the kingdom of heaven."	We are "poor in spirit" when we depend on God and make God more important than anyone or anything else in our lives.
"Blessed are they who mourn, for they will be comforted."	We "mourn" when we are sad because of the selfish ways people treat each other.
"Blessed are the meek, for they will inherit the land."	We are "meek" when we are patient, kind, and respectful to all people, even those who do not respect us.
"Blessed are they who hunger and thirst for righteousness, for they will be satisfied."	We "hunger and thirst for righteousness" when we search for justice and treat everyone fairly.
"Blessed are the merciful, for they will be shown mercy."	We are "merciful" when we forgive others and do not take revenge on those who hurt us.
"Blessed are the clean of heart, for they will see God."	We are "clean of heart" when we are faithful to God's teachings and try to see God in all people and all situations.
"Blessed are the peacemakers, for they will be called children of God."	We are "peacemakers" when we treat others with love and respect and when we help others to stop fighting and make peace.
"Blessed are they who are persecuted for the sake of righteousness, for theirs is the kingdom of heaven." Matthew 5:3–10	We are "persecuted for the sake of righteousness" when others disrespect us for living as disciples of Jesus and following his example.

Parish page 269 / School page 349

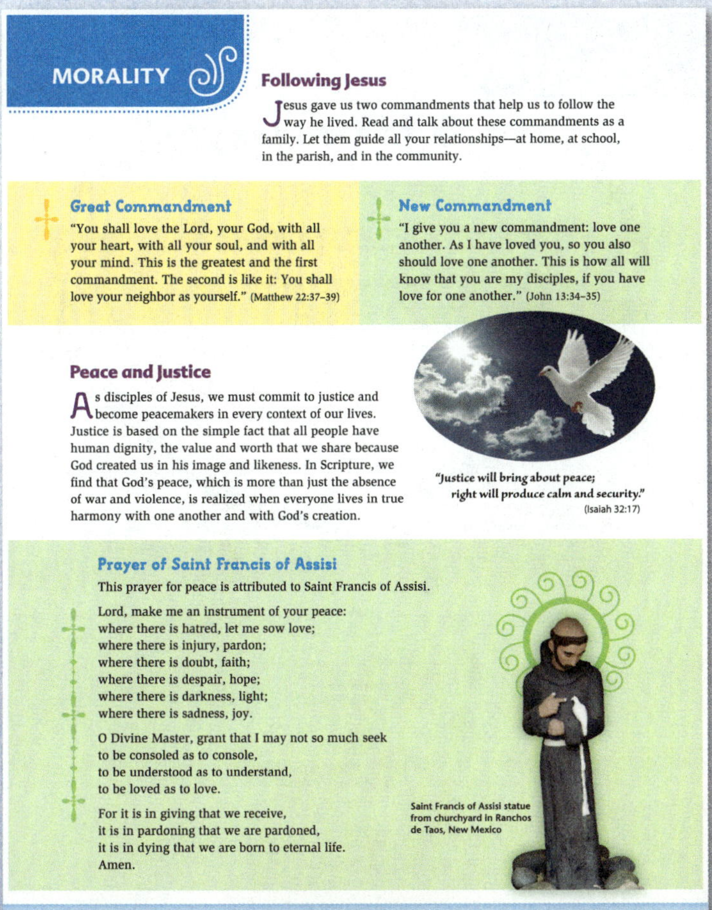

MORALITY

Following Jesus

Jesus gave us two commandments that help us to follow the way he lived. Read and talk about these commandments as a family. Let them guide all your relationships—at home, at school, in the parish, and in the community.

Great Commandment
"You shall love the Lord, your God, with all your heart, with all your soul, and with all your mind. This is the greatest and the first commandment. The second is like it: You shall love your neighbor as yourself." (Matthew 22:37–39)

New Commandment
"I give you a new commandment: love one another. As I have loved you, so you also should love one another. This is how all will know that you are my disciples, if you have love for one another." (John 13:34–35)

Peace and Justice

As disciples of Jesus, we must commit to justice and become peacemakers in every context of our lives. Justice is based on the simple fact that all people have human dignity, the value and worth that we share because God created us in his image and likeness. In Scripture, we find that God's peace, which is more than just the absence of war and violence, is realized when everyone lives in true harmony with one another and with God's creation.

"Justice will bring about peace; right will produce calm and security." (Isaiah 32:17)

Prayer of Saint Francis of Assisi

This prayer for peace is attributed to Saint Francis of Assisi.

Lord, make me an instrument of your peace:
where there is hatred, let me sow love;
where there is injury, pardon;
where there is doubt, faith;
where there is despair, hope;
where there is darkness, light;
where there is sadness, joy.

O Divine Master, grant that I may not so much seek
to be consoled as to console,
to be understood as to understand,
to be loved as to love.

For it is in giving that we receive,
it is in pardoning that we are pardoned,
it is in dying that we are born to eternal life.
Amen.

Saint Francis of Assisi statue from churchyard in Ranchos de Taos, New Mexico

Parish page 270 / School page 350

MORALITY

A Roadmap to Happiness

Familiarize the children with this section before they share it at home, reading to them the Beatitudes from Matthew 5:3–10. Review that the word *blessed* in the Beatitudes means "happy." The Beatitudes are a promise of God's blessings. Jesus explained that by living according to the Beatitudes, we can help spread God's Kingdom, and, in turn, we can find true happiness.

Following Jesus

Encourage the children to introduce this section to their families by sharing that Jesus was the perfect example of loving God and others.

Great Commandment

Explain that when Jesus was asked what commandment of God's law was the greatest, he responded with the words from Matthew 22:37–39 shown on the page. Jesus' response is known as the Great Commandment. Encourage the children to read these words with their families.

New Commandment

Invite the children to review with their families the New Commandment that Jesus gave us, which teaches us to love as he did. Invite the children to discuss with their families some ways they can show love following the Great Commandment and the New Commandment.

Peace and Justice

Prepare the children to share this section at home by explaining to them that human dignity is the value and worth that come from being made in God's image. Jesus upheld the dignity and rights of every human person. Jesus' life and teaching call us to work for justice and peace.

Prayer of Saint Francis of Assisi

Review the information about Saint Francis of Assisi from "Saint Stories" in *Project Disciple* at the end of Chapter 1 in the student book. You may wish to have the children practice praying the Prayer of Saint Francis of Assisi before sharing it at home.

PRAYER

Praying the Rosary

Encourage the children to share this section with their families. Show the children rosary beads. Explain that the Rosary is a special prayer in honor of Mary. Explain that when we pray the Rosary, we use the beads as we pray.

Mysteries of the Rosary

Tell the children that the Mysteries of the Rosary recall special times in the lives of Jesus and Mary. We think about these Mysteries as we pray using each set of ten beads.

The Rosary

Demonstrate praying the Rosary for the class following the steps on the page. Point out the prayers we say on the different beads. We begin with the Sign of the Cross, the Apostles' Creed, Our Father, three Hail Marys, and a Glory Be to the Father. Then there are five sets of ten beads to pray Hail Marys. Each set begins with the Our Father and ends with the Glory Be to the Father. Each set of prayers using ten beads is called a decade.

Have the children practice praying one decade of the Rosary with you. Introduce the decade by announcing the first Joyful Mystery, the Annunciation (see Luke 1:26–38). Invite the children to think about this event while praying the decade.

Invite the children to make sure the family has rosary beads they can use to complete the steps on the page at home. (You might send home a set of rosary beads for each family or have the children check in advance for rosary beads at home that may be used.)

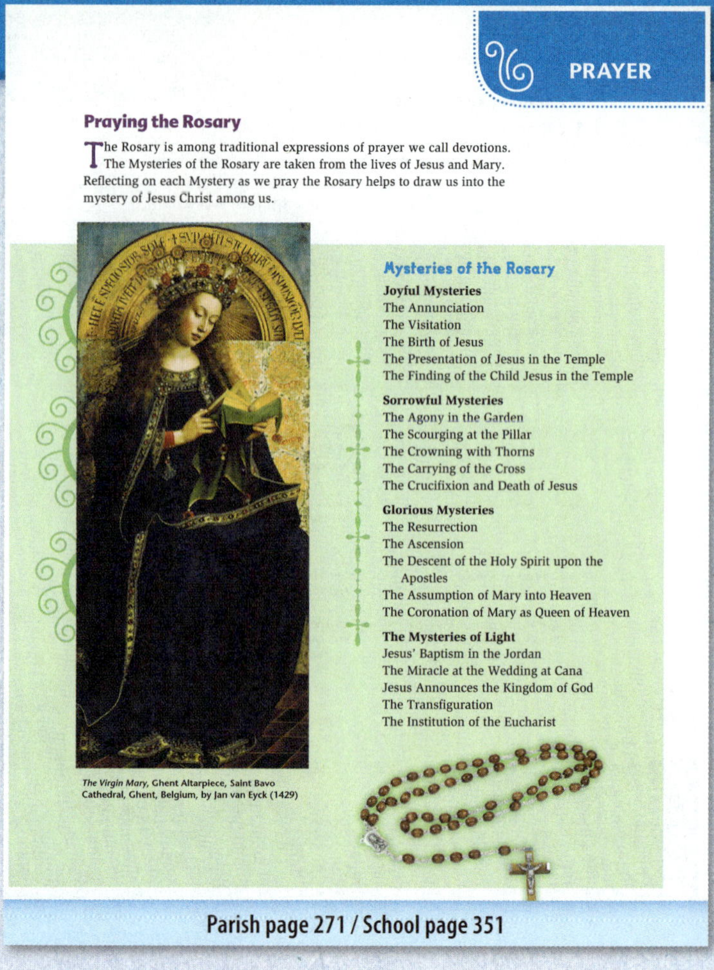

PRAYER

Praying the Rosary

The Rosary is among traditional expressions of prayer we call devotions. The Mysteries of the Rosary are taken from the lives of Jesus and Mary. Reflecting on each Mystery as we pray the Rosary helps to draw us into the mystery of Jesus Christ among us.

The Virgin Mary, Ghent Altarpiece, Saint Bavo Cathedral, Ghent, Belgium, by Jan van Eyck (1429)

Mysteries of the Rosary

Joyful Mysteries
The Annunciation
The Visitation
The Birth of Jesus
The Presentation of Jesus in the Temple
The Finding of the Child Jesus in the Temple

Sorrowful Mysteries
The Agony in the Garden
The Scourging at the Pillar
The Crowning with Thorns
The Carrying of the Cross
The Crucifixion and Death of Jesus

Glorious Mysteries
The Resurrection
The Ascension
The Descent of the Holy Spirit upon the Apostles
The Assumption of Mary into Heaven
The Coronation of Mary as Queen of Heaven

The Mysteries of Light
Jesus' Baptism in the Jordan
The Miracle at the Wedding at Cana
Jesus Announces the Kingdom of God
The Transfiguration
The Institution of the Eucharist

Parish page 271 / School page 351

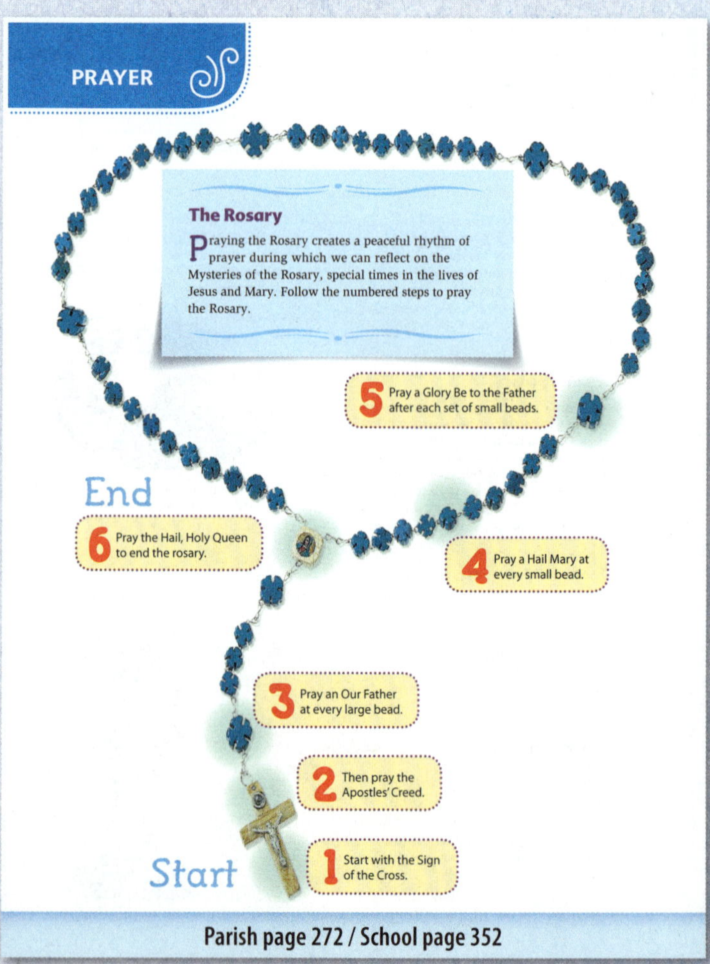

PRAYER

The Rosary

Praying the Rosary creates a peaceful rhythm of prayer during which we can reflect on the Mysteries of the Rosary, special times in the lives of Jesus and Mary. Follow the numbered steps to pray the Rosary.

Parish page 272 / School page 352

Catholic Identity Retreat

Meditation: Trust in God

This meditation can be used for any retreat. Read the meditation aloud to settle the children:

Close your eyes. Listen to this reading from the Book of Psalms in the Bible. Think about what the words mean. (*Pause.*)

"Answer when I call, my saving God.
In my troubles, you cleared a way;
show me favor; hear my prayer." (*Pause.*)

"Know that the LORD works wonders for the faithful;
the LORD hears when I call out." (*Pause.*)

". . . you alone, LORD, make me secure." (Psalm 4:2, 4, 9)

Now, silently pray in your own words. Trust that God hears and answers your prayer.

RETREAT ENERGIZER: Participation in the Mass

The Book of Psalms is a collection of poetic prayers and songs in the Old Testament of the Bible. The psalms help us to give worship to God. They are an important part of the Church's liturgy. Display the Responsorial Psalm for this Sunday's Mass for the children. Encourage the children to read or sing the Responsorial Psalm.

Catholic Identity Retreat

Handout A Prayer in Time of Need

Write your own short prayer to God. Include words about trusting God to help with our needs.

Catholic Identity Retreat

Recipe and Table Blessing

Vegetable Salad

1 bunch broccoli, cut into chunks

1 head cauliflower, cut into chunks

1 cucumber, diced

1 cup crumbled feta cheese

$\frac{1}{4}$ cup red onion, diced

1 cup raisins or sliced strawberries

1 cup raspberry vinaigrette dressing

Combine broccoli, cauliflower, cucumber, feta cheese, and red onion. Coat with raspberry vinaigrette dressing, stirring. Just before serving, sprinkle with raisins or strawberries. Serves 18.

Use this recipe to prepare for an extended retreat that includes a meal. Use the table blessing during this extended retreat.

Visit **religion.sadlierconnect.com** for more resources to extend your retreats.

Table Blessing

Bless us and this food of our retreat.
As we gather at the table,
may we appreciate and celebrate
the gift of Jesus Christ, the Son of God,
and imitate his example of loving service.
Amen.

Acknowledgments

Excerpts from the English translation of the *Catechism of the Catholic Church* for the United States of America, copyright © 1994, United States Catholic Conference, Inc.—Libreria Editrice Vaticana. English translation of the *Catechism of the Catholic Church: Modifications from the Editio Typica* copyright © 1997, United States Catholic Conference, Inc.—Libreria Editrice Vaticana. Used with permission.

Scripture excerpts are taken from the *New American Bible with Revised New Testament and Psalms* Copyright © 1991, 1986, 1970, Confraternity of Christian Doctrine, Inc., Washington, D.C. Used with permission. All rights reserved. No part of the *New American Bible* may be reproduced by any means without permission in writing from the copyright owner.

Excerpt from the English translation of *Rite of Baptism for Children* © 1969, International Committee on English in the Liturgy, Inc. All rights reserved.

Photo Credits

Cover: SuperStock/Richard Cummins: *Cathedral of the Madeleine, Salt Lake City, Utah*. Interior: Neal Farris: 33. Getty Images/Ariel Skelley: xii. Used under license from Shutterstock.com/ORLIO: 35; pavelena: 33 *background*. SuperStock/Blend Images/Jon Feingersh: iv.

Illustrator Credit

Series Patterned Background Design: Evan Polenghi.